SO, YOU WANT TO BE A WRITER?

Ian Carroll

Oakamoor
Publishing

Published in 2020 by Oakamoor Publishing, an imprint of Bennion Kearny Limited.

Copyright © Oakamoor Publishing

ISBN: 978-1-910773-71-0

Ian Carroll has asserted his right under the Copyright, Designs and Patents Act, 1988 to be identified as the author of this book.

All Rights Reserved. No part of this publication may be reproduced, stored in a retrieval system, or transmitted in any form or by any means, electronic, mechanical, photocopying, recording or otherwise, without the prior permission of the publisher.

This book is sold subject to the condition that it shall not, by way of trade or otherwise, be lent, re-sold, hired out or otherwise circulated without the publisher's prior consent in any form of binding or cover other than that it which it is published and without a similar condition including this condition being imposed on the subsequent purchaser.

Bennion Kearny has endeavoured to provide trademark information about all the companies and products mentioned in this book by the appropriate use of capitals. However, Bennion Kearny cannot guarantee the accuracy of this information.

Published by Oakamoor Publishing, Bennion Kearny Limited
6 Woodside
Churnet View Road
Oakamoor
Staffordshire
ST10 3AE

www.BennionKearny.com

'This book is dedicated to Lucas McCall.

Welcome to the world, little cousin.

May all your dreams come true.

TABLE OF CONTENTS

PROLOGUE 1

INTRODUCTION 2

THE WRITING GAME 3
MONEY VERSUS ART 5
TO BE A WRITER 7
THE OPTIONS 10
MY CREDENTIALS 13
STARTING OUT 17
FEEDBACK 20
WRITING COURSES 24
WRITING QUALIFICATIONS 27
PROFESSIONAL ADVICE 29
THE STORYTELLER'S CRAFT 32
JOSEPH CAMPBELL 35
HOW TO WRITE A PLAY 38
THE PLAYWRIGHT AS PRODUCER 42
HOW TO ADAPT A PLAY 45
FROM WHERE COMES INSPIRATION? 49
GET YOURSELF ON A SHELF 54
HOW TO WRITE A BOOK 57
HOW TO WRITE FICTION 60
HOW TO WRITE NON-FICTION 67
HOW TO WRITE A MEMOIR 70
HOW TO WRITE A BIOGRAPHY 74
HOW TO WRITE A MANUAL 77
HOW TO WRITE IN 'FREE-FLOW' 80
HOW TO BE A GHOST-WRITER 82

EACH FORMAT IS A DIFFERENT LANGUAGE 86
SCREENWRITING. PART ONE 88
SCREENWRITING. PART TWO 92
SCREENWRITING. PART THREE 96
THE DIFFERENCE BETWEEN FILM AND TV WRITING 101
HOW TO ADAPT A BOOK 104
OTHER AVENUES 107
WRITING FOR TELEVISION 110
THE WRITING DAY 113
WRITING IS A LONELY BUSINESS 116
DAYDREAMING. THE BEST PART 119
HOW TO GET AN AGENT 122
HOW TO GET A PUBLISHER 126
SELF-PUBLISHING 128
LEARN TO TYPE 131
THE WRITER'S GUILD. YOUR UNION 133
COPYRIGHT. PROTECT YOURSELF 134
TWENTY YEARS TO BECOME AN OVERNIGHT SUCCESS 136
SO YOU WANT TO RETIRE EARLY? 138
MARKETING YOURSELF AND YOUR WORK 139

CONCLUSION 142

PROLOGUE

So you want to be a writer? I'm guessing you do because either you, or someone close to you who supports your ambition, has purchased this book. So I guess that you want to be a writer.

Within these pages, you will find advice and encouragement, helpful tips and commentary, about what it is to be – and to want to be – a writer.

We'll cover a range of topics, from writing fiction and non-fiction, theatrical plays (both original and adaptations), as well as screenplays, and many of the other forms that writing can take. We'll discuss different genres, formats for writing, obstacles to overcome, and also explore the many avenues that will hopefully lead you to success.

Most of all, you will get my unbridled passion for the subject – for *our* subject – that can inspire you to go on and achieve your dream.

And it is a dream, because writing is a calling. It's not just a job. To be a writer is to be an artist, a creative, a painter in words not pictures. It is both demanding and rewarding. It is a craft that has to be learned, and only then can any talent that you possess come to the fore.

So let's go and have some fun, learn a few things, and help you on your way to becoming a writer. That's what you want. I want it for you too. So let's do it!

INTRODUCTION

Across this book, I'll be your guide, your tutor, if you like. As such, I think it's only right that I should explain my credentials for the role.

At the time of writing, I am 53 years of age, and I've shared the same goal as you for the last 30 years of my life. Prior to that, I always felt that I had a calling. The only problem was, I had no idea what that calling was.

Eventually, I had my 'light bulb' moment. I was writing poetry. Couldn't help myself, it just came pouring out of me, and I realised that what I really wanted to do, more than anything else in the world, was to be a storyteller.

The easiest way for me to do that, as I sure as heck couldn't draw or paint, was to be a writer. As soon as I said those magical words, 'I want to be a writer', everything fell into place for me. I knew that I had found my calling.

That's not to say that I became a writer overnight, or that all I have done ever since is tell stories for the past three decades. No, I have a job. I write in my spare time. But along the way, I have earned a Master's degree in writing, and I have self-published two works of fiction and four of non-fiction.

I have also recently acquired three book publishing deals with professional publishing houses and, in 2019, one of them, 'Cooperman! The life of Tommy Cooper', was a *Daily Mail* book of the week.

I have also written, directed, and produced three original plays for the stage, and adapted three others based on literary classics. I've even written and produced a Christmas Panto. These plays have been performed the length and breadth of the country to critical and audience acclaim.

My first screenplay was twice optioned in 2001, and I have since written over a dozen more, with one currently in development as a major television series.

In all, I have written, and written, and then written some more, in a variety of genres and for a variety of different media.

Now, I'd like to share my experience and knowledge with you.

As I wrote in the introduction to my first published work, *A 4000 year history of Israel and Palestine*, 'It promises to be some journey. I hope you'll come with me.'

I hope that all of you budding writers will do the same.

THE WRITING GAME

When we say the words 'I want to be a writer', we are saying that we want to spend our days employed in the craft of communication via the written word. I'm sure that most of us, and most lay-people, imagine that this means staring out of the window (with that window preferably overlooking a fabulous bay on some beautiful or rugged coastline). Then, when inspiration strikes, we act as conduits as the words pour out of us until – some time later – a work of genius emerges that will be adored by the masses and will make us the envy of our peers.

Fame may follow, though not everyone who writes wants that particular millstone. Fortune may follow, and I'm sure that most of us wouldn't say no to that. However, what you will probably end up with is an interesting hobby, a second-income if you're lucky, and also a real enhancement of your spiritual and mental well-being. To do something that you love brings a whole host of benefits that you won't have considered when all you knew was that you wanted to be a writer.

The truth is, very few of us writers hit the jackpot. Many make a career out of it in journalism or in some other avenue of the arts, but picking up a pen or sitting down at a computer to write, is about as likely to earn you financial reward as is buying a metal detector and heading out to your nearest beach or field on a weekend.

We write because we want to, or feel that we have to, and not because we expect to get rich beyond our wildest dreams.

So what is the writing game? It is to sit your bum down on a chair and pour words out onto a journal or computer. It is to give up countless hours – precious time that you could have spent watching TV or socialising, or learning French, or canoodling on the sofa with your partner, or playing with your kids, or visiting with your family, or watching your favourite football team (or whatever sport you follow), or pursuing whichever hobby you enjoy.

It is to be *dedicated* beyond all reason in your passion to share stories with others, in whichever medium (books, screenplays, etc.) you choose. The idea that comes to you, or that you work hard to generate, will usually lend itself more to one medium than another. You will make that choice either on your own preferences or skillset, or as determined by the facets of that particular idea.

Does your idea work better as a film script, as a play, or as a book? Maybe musicality is in the air, in which case you could have a musical or even an opera on your hands. The idea may simply make a good joke or comedy sketch, and *that* might be the extent of *that* particular invention.

Whatever it is, it's your job to decide, and your job to sit down and write it. Because, if you don't commit it to paper or craft a document out of it, how is it ever going to exist? You're a creator. Create. You're a writer. Write.

I once spent three months in the South of France. I'd taken a little time off work (because I could just about afford to), and I went with no other idea than to learn a bit of the language and to do a bit of writing. Whenever I wondered what exactly I was doing there, and how I would be viewed by the locals, the writing always gave me most pride in who I was, and what I was doing.

In every guide book and in every gallery that I visited, they eulogised about the famous artists and writers who had spent time in their home town. These were their most esteemed sons and daughters, and I was merely the latest incarnation of a creative in their midst. The place also inspired my two works of fiction, something that I hadn't expected when I went there. Inspiration, for a writer, can come from anywhere and at any time.

So, to be a writer is to dip your toe into a creative pool and to offer up something a little bit special to the world. It is to be prepared to be the one who holds court, to tell the story, and the cardinal rule is that you need to *hold your audience's attention*. Storytelling is one of the things that holds humanity together, and its tradition goes back to the very beginning of mankind.

Can anyone be a writer? Well, anyone can write, but that doesn't mean that you have the storytelling gift. I recently read an interview with a screenwriter who said that in order to be a writer, you should be able to tell a good anecdote. Is that you?

If you can tell a good joke or a good anecdote, I think you therefore possess the required rhythm, timing, and eye for detail that a good writer should have. So, if that sounds like you, I'd say you have the core ingredients.

To that, I would add that you must also be a self-starter, able to work alone, to be disciplined, and have the persistence to pursue your goal to the sweet or bitter end. Have you got that innate ability and the willpower to see it through?

If so, then great!

Welcome to the writing game!

MONEY VERSUS ART

Do we write for money or for the sake of art? I would suggest that anyone who sets out to write purely for money is the most misguided of our tribe. There are no guarantees, and I would say that you are going to put yourself under enormous pressure to write something commercial and, in doing so, that you will miss out on the apprenticeship that you must endure and also enjoy.

There is a quote from a famous author that goes 'Anyone who writes for anything other than money is an ass', or words to that effect. For 29 out of the 30 years that I've been writing, I would have disagreed. I wrote sometimes for 12 hours a day, seven days a week, unprompted and unpaid. And I never batted an eye-lid. If I was ever going to make it as a writer, I just saw it as serving my time.

I wrote stories that I was dying to tell, and gained huge satisfaction from seeing plays performed in public, hearing audiences laughing at jokes that never existed until I put them on a page and into the mouths of actors. I wrote because I wanted to, because I loved it, and because I had to. I was a writer. It was what I was born to do.

But, in the past two years, I've earned three book publishing deals. It's like the door to success has finally opened. And I honestly wouldn't mind a bit of financial reward for all of that time and effort. It would be nice, that's all.

Am I still an artist? As much as ever, I'd say. Do I think I should be paid for my work? Well, if there's any going, I'll have some of it, thank you very much.

But these are arguments for a later day. First of all, writing, and being a writer, is very much its own reward. If you set out to write for money, I think that way misery lies. If you write simply to tell stories, then I think that way happiness lies.

You want your stories to be heard, and you want to tell them in the most interesting and exciting way that you can. That should be your goal and your focus.

First of all, you are going to have a very long apprenticeship ahead of you. Think ten years minimum. Personally, I got myself a good day job because I thought it might be 20 years before I got my break. If I had known that it would take me close to 30 before I even got a sniff, well, I may have been a little downhearted. But, keep learning, keep knocking at the door. When you're ready, it will open.

Do you want to spend the interim period writing stuff you can sell, or stories that you love? I would argue the latter. You need that passion to sustain you in the endeavour. You have a lot to learn. We'll discuss the ways you can go about that within the pages of this book.

So, money versus art. A fork in the road. And which to choose? Choose art. The money will follow eventually if you keep going for long enough and write stuff of sufficient quality. And, if it doesn't? Well, you knew it was going to take time, so you got on with your life anyway, didn't you? You valued your friends and your family. You found a companion, maybe raised a family. Went to work, were nice to your colleagues, helped old ladies across the street, and cheered on your local football team.

Your life was enhanced by the fact that you had an outlet, a conduit to the world, in which you told stories. Maybe it will eventually pay off for you. You might get an annual holiday out of the proceeds, which isn't a bad bonus. Or maybe you'll earn enough to give up the day job and live the life that you really want to lead. You may even earn more money than you need. Wouldn't that be something? But if you don't write for art, and write from the heart, I think that most people setting out on our journey will have a more difficult and less rewarding time along the way.

Roger Corman – king of the low-budget movie – and a particular hero of mine, once said, 'What have you got to show for shuffling papers in an office for 40 years aside from a huge stack of invoices? When you make a movie (or in our case, write a play, screenplay, or novel), at least there is tangible proof of your existence. You create something. At the beginning, there is nothing. Then you get an idea. And at the end is a story with a beginning, middle, and end.'

I think that sums it up pretty neatly. Write because you have to. Create. Be an artist. If the money comes, great. If not, you will still have something to show for all of your effort. You told stories.

So, if you want to be a writer, your audience is waiting to hear the story that you, the writer, desperately want to share with the world.

At this stage of your career, choose art over money. When you've earned your stripes, you'll know where the money is, but you'll never get there unless you begin by creating art. That's your first duty, to yourself and the waiting world.

You're an artist first and foremost. Whether you end up a rich one or not remains to be seen.

TO BE A WRITER

To be a writer is to set yourself apart. You are going to find a unique viewpoint and record your experiences or ideas. You are going to look for new and exciting ways to engage an audience. And, you are going to do it of your own volition, as a self-starter.

When I first embarked on this path of being a writer, I wondered what kind of reception I might get when I announced my calling to the world. I have to say, I have been pleasantly surprised.

Writers seem to arouse people's curiosity and, overwhelmingly, the reaction I have received has been positive. The most common response you will hear is, 'You should write my book'. Everyone seems to think that their own lives are unbelievable. And quite often, they are right!

'You couldn't write it' is another expression that we all use. Well, in our case, we have to!

My response, whenever people ask me to write their book, is this.

'I'm busy. Write your own book!'

I say this as nicely as possible, of course, but there is a great deal of truth in the statement.

Because here's the thing. It's not easy to give up your free time to write about *anything*, least of all someone else's story that you have no affinity with, and probably no passion for. It's hard enough to write the story that *you* are passionate about. Anything else is a non-starter. Again, art should take precedence over money (although there are exceptions to every rule).

Another Roger, this time Moore, not Corman, once explained away some of the poor movie-choices he'd made as an actor throughout his career. Well, he'd occasionally experienced a bit of 'resting' between acting gigs, therefore he'd been given the advice to take pretty much everything that was offered to him because, if he wasn't acting, then he wasn't really an actor.

I'd say the same is true for us. If we want to call ourselves writers, then we must write. Never mind if it never sees the light of day, or it never gets published or produced. It's either part of your development or it's your breakthrough script.

To be a writer, you have to write. Otherwise, what are you? A shopkeeper, a school teacher, a surveyor? Nothing wrong with any of that. My wife is a shopkeeper. My sister is a school teacher. I am a surveyor. But I'm only a writer when I write.

You can afford yourself a little time off between writing gigs. Write one script or one novel a year, take a couple of months off, and then write another. Do so consistently, over a ten year period (or whatever), and you could still call yourself a writer, but if you wrote only one thing a few years ago, and you've written nothing since, can you still call yourself a writer? I don't think so. So get writing.

Besides, like with anything, the more you write, the better you'll get at it, and the greater will be your chances of ultimate success.

There is an old adage that, to be considered a master of anything, you need to put in 10,000 hours of practice. If you write one hour a day after work, from Monday to Friday, that's only 250 hours a year. By that definition, it would take you 40 years to master your craft. I don't think any of us really want or expect to have to wait that long to achieve a modicum of success, therefore I suggest that you try to increase your output. Maybe write for two hours a day. Maybe put in a bit of a shift over a weekend. Basically, write *whenever* and *wherever* possible. That way, you'll reach that 10,000 hour mark a whole lot quicker.

Stephen King, in his book, *On Writing*, says that to be a writer, you must also be a reader. Who am I to argue? I'd also go as far as to say that whatever it is that you like to read, or whichever type of plays or films you like to watch, then *that* particular field is probably where your own writing belongs. Because you'll understand the medium.

If all you read and enjoy are crime thrillers, you should attempt one of those.

The Scottish actor Brian Cox was the first person to portray Hannibal Lecter on screen. When the franchise was picked up by the Hollywood big-wigs, they ditched Brian – as excellent as he was and is – and opted for Anthony Hopkins instead.

Mr. Cox lamented his fortunes to a friend.

'I get parts, but never the big parts, or the best parts. There's always someone more famous that they want for the role, building on all the good work that I've put in beforehand.'

You can understand his frustration.

The response he received was a good one. His friend advised that he shouldn't be bothered about any of that. He shouldn't try to join the A-list, or even the A-plus-list. All he should be interested in was doing good work. Consistent good work. He might also have added, 'and keep working'.

I think that's good advice. *You can't chase fame or fortune.* It's in the lap of the Gods as to who gets what and when. We're all meant to get our 15 minutes anyway.

Better to just get your head down and concentrate on producing good work. That way, you'll be serving your apprenticeship, accruing your ten thousand hours. And you'll be writing, which is what makes you, yes you, a writer.

THE OPTIONS

What sort of a writer do you want to be? In which field do you want to work? We're going to concentrate on the areas of novel writing, playwriting, and screenwriting. These are the areas where I have gained my experience, and are therefore the ones that I feel most qualified to discuss. We'll also touch on fields such as journalism and writing for radio, but an oft-quoted adage for writers is to *write what you know*.

You're going to be pigeon-holed by audiences and critics at some point in your career. Step out of the box you've been placed in, and you may well find yourself being called a hybrid-author. That's why, even when someone as esteemed as JK Rowling decides to try her hand at something different, she'll write under another name. And that's just for a book in a different genre. What happens if you're a novelist who wants to write a play, or a screenwriter who wants to write a novel?

The answer is to serve your apprenticeship and write the story that you want to in the medium that best serves that particular story. Obviously, if you've served your 10,000-hour apprenticeship as a playwright, it is quite disheartening to think you'd have to do it all again just because you want to write a book.

The good news is, you will have gathered a great deal of transferable writing skills, and you will probably have dabbled in several of these areas anyway as you went about the business of learning your craft.

We're going to cover many of your options within the pages of this book, and this will hopefully help you decide which area suits you best, and how to move between the particular fields.

As with Stephen King's advice to be a reader if you want to be a writer, I would say the same thing is true if you want to be a screenwriter, to write for television, or to be a playwright. The good news is that all that time spent watching your favourite television soap counts towards your 10,000 hours. You may have to concentrate a little harder, and you may lose a little of the satisfaction you get by just 'switching off' and relaxing and enjoying your favourite show, but it's not the worst bit of work you'll ever do either, reclining on the sofa and letting it all soak in.

Assuming you're just embarking on your goal of being a writer, or you're at an early-ish stage of your journey, then what exactly are your options?

Well, the first thing to decide is how you are going to live. Are you going to get a day job to pay the rent (or mortgage) and the bills, to put food in the cupboards, clothes on your back, and whatever little treats in life you allow yourself? If so, what sort of job are you going to try and get? It must be one that allows you the time and energy to write around the demands of the day job. I would suggest, therefore, that you shouldn't go into something too exacting, like being a junior doctor, working 12-hour shifts at the local hospital, leaving you physically and mentally drained at the end of each day. When on earth would you write?

Should you just jump straight in and find a role within the arts, even if it's just something administrative and pitched at a fairly low level? That's not actually a bad shout. You will probably get to see the creative process in action, and you'll pick up some valuable tips along the way.

Personally, I decided to go down the route of being a quantity surveyor. It's largely maths-based. The way I saw it, if I was working with numbers all day, I wouldn't have used up that creative part of the brain I would need when I sat down to write every night.

So, assuming that you've decided how you're going to balance the act of living while pursuing your dream of being a writer, what choices are available to you now?

If you want to be a journalist, you could do a degree in the subject and try to get taken on by one of the small regional papers. That way, you'll be learning and earning at the same time.

If you want to be a playwright, you could see if there are any courses or workshops run by your local theatre. You could volunteer to help them out, maybe as an usher, and pick the brains of any playwrights that you come across. Personally, I was Script Editor for a play that won my local paper's Best Writing award. For 12 months, I attended every rehearsal and every performance.

I worked on someone else's script, making small changes and carrying out additional research, then worked closely with the actors to help them learn their lines and adapt to any changes. It was an intimate, behind-the-scenes exposure to seeing a script come to life. So much so that – three years later – I felt suitably qualified to write, direct, and produce my own work for the stage.

If you want to write for television, you need to study the craft and write a sample script, all of which will be talked about within the pages of this book. You can submit your sample script to writing competitions or to places such as the BBC's Writers Room, which regularly accepts unsolicited scripts. Their website will also alert you to other writing opportunities, and you can submit everything from full-length feature films to short comedy sketches.

You're going to need that sample script to be stand-out smart, otherwise it's going to be swiftly rejected. It's unlikely that the first thing you write (or even the tenth!) is going to be great. What you need at this stage is feedback. Don't give it to your mum. Have a think. Do you know any actors, or anyone remotely involved in film, television, or theatre, who may have some knowledge of how a script works?

If so, ask whether they would mind taking a look at your script and giving you some honest feedback. And that's the thing. It must be honest. And you must take on the chin any criticism that they give you. Don't try and defend it. It's not their fault that they didn't like it or that they didn't understand it. You just haven't written a good enough script yet. You're still learning. And the learning and development that you need will not take place if you don't find people to read your work or if you don't embrace any remarks that they give you. Trust me, when you eventually get a script returned with a note saying that they quite enjoyed it, you'll feel like a million dollars. And you will be well on your way to being the writer that you want to be.

The same is true for screenplays. Try to get them into the hands of literary agents and film producers, but also into the hands of actors. That's a good place to start. Again, don't fire until you're ready. Get a good sample script written before you make your approach. How will you know when it's good? Well, your first readers will tell you, and you should be improving with every script that you write, so keep writing.

Maybe you see your future as a novelist or non-fiction writer. You're probably going to study a degree in English (or in whichever area, such as History, you see yourself writing about). Many people harbour dreams of being a successful author. Very few can actually claim to be such a thing. There's a lot of competition. Study, learn, write. And persevere. It's a popular dream, and the prize is not given away lightly.

The good news is, with the internet and the eBook revolution, it's never been easier to see your name in print. But, while it's never been easier to get your work out there, it's as hard as it ever was to make a success of it.

Marketing can help, once you have a saleable product, but ultimately your audience will decide how much time they want to spend with you and how much of their money they want to give you.

There are many choices for the type of writer that you can be, and there is no bar to moving between the different writing forms. The duty you have, and the responsibility that you have to yourself is to give of your best in order to achieve your goal. Write often. Write well. And keep believing.

MY CREDENTIALS

I started out writing poetry. I even did a bit of stand-up comedy. I did lots of gigs as a performance poet, and I was a truly awful stand-up. Then I got an idea that I thought would make for a good short film. I searched for a book on scriptwriting in my local library (this was all before the internet sprung to life), and I learned how to set out a script.

I started to write my first script, having no idea what I was really doing. I gave names to the characters, and then I got them to perform whatever actions they needed to do as they set about achieving their goals.

Before too long, I had a finished script. At the time, I was working on the restoration of the Albert Memorial in London, my first job since graduating as a surveyor. One day, Lord Snowdon arrived at the monument to do a photoshoot with Alan Rickman, the distinguished British actor.

I chose a moment and approached the two men, introduced myself, and asked Mr. Rickman if he'd be kind enough to read my short film script. He laughed knowingly. Was there no place he could go without someone shoving a script in his hand?

Graciously, he said yes and, a couple of days later, I received a handwritten letter from him critiquing my script. He began by saying that it had a lot of energy and atmosphere. The rest of the letter was a very long 'but' where he pointed out my maiden script's many faults. He then wished me luck with my writing, *and* with the Albert Memorial. In other words, don't give up the day job!

I then decided to write a novel. Autobiographical, of course. The sort of very early introspective coming-of-age story that I think most of us – maybe you included – will probably write on your own writer's journey.

Before we completed the restoration of the Albert Memorial, we decided to place a time capsule two-thirds of the way up the monument behind one of the ornate panels. I placed a copy of my autobiographical manuscript inside the time capsule for future generations to one-day find and revere my undoubted and, at the time, undiscovered genius.

When I told a mate (one of the few to have read it) that I had sealed my novel inside a box, hidden behind a panel, 100 feet up in the air, thereby secreting it from public view for the next 100 years, he said 'Best place for it!'

I guess I still had a lot to learn.

I had an idea for another book. I planned to take three months off work to write it. The Albert Memorial now complete, I moved back home and stayed with my parents while I wrote book number two.

Then, an actor friend of mine got a part in a play. They needed a script editor. The subject was very close to my heart. I got the job. I spent a year attending rehearsals and working on the script and the play, working with actors, watching them rehearse and perform. It was a valuable lesson in an area of the arts in which I had zero experience up to that point.

I then began writing screenplays. My second novel, a childhood memoir, I thought had the potential to be a film. Now that I knew a few actors, I thought I could write a feature-length script. Again, I started to study the format.

When I was in London, I had been a member of the London Screenwriter's Workshop. I attended many different seminars and undertook several courses. I also went regularly to the cinema.

It was the age of Oasis, of Tarantino, of *Trainspotting*, and Irvine Welsh. Culture got a little closer to home for a working-class Northern lad like myself.

And I kept writing. I wrote maybe five feature-length screenplays. I got a copy of the *Writers' and Artists' Yearbook*. You should do the same. Put it on your Christmas list if budgets are tight.

I sent those early film scripts to agents and film producers. I gave them to my actor friends to read. One day, I got a letter back from an agent. He said he thought that the script based on my childhood was both amusing and poignant, but he didn't think he could do much with it. But – and here was the compliment – he said I could send him other scripts in the future.

Here's the thing. You should always keep writing. That, in itself, is a sign that you are serious about the whole thing. It can take months and months for these people to reply. Don't wait by the phone. Keep writing.

When the bloke said 'Send me your next one', little did he know that he would receive it in the next post!

I then had a screenplay twice optioned by a film producer of some renown. I earned my first money from writing when he gave me £100 for the option on my script, and another £100 when he took up the option again six months later.

I signed a contract with him that would have seen me jet around the world at his company's expense should they ever find the money to actually make the film. The project ultimately went nowhere (which happens maybe 99 times out of a 100 with this sort of thing), but it was a validation of sorts. I was on my way.

Then came my first theatrical play, which was written, directed, and produced by myself. I'd read a book many years before that I thought would make a great play. The only problem was, I didn't know how to write a play. But, emboldened by my work as a script editor, and with my previous screenwriting experience, I sat down and wrote my first piece for the stage.

I sent it to a small but prestigious local theatre, asking if they'd like to put it on. They said that it was good, but that they weren't in the habit of putting other people's plays on. They were a venue for hire, basically. So, I asked the obvious question, 'How much is it to hire the place?'

Nine months after I first sat down and stared at the blank piece of paper that would become page one of the script, I stood on stage amongst my actors enjoying a standing ovation from a sell-out audience. One of the best feelings ever. And I could *still* remember staring at that initial blank page.

You'll have your own journey too, and your own magical days, I hope.

Then I did a Master's degree in Writing. It gave me a writing focus one day a week. It meant that I was keeping my hand in. And I learned a lot. I always thought that I would make it as a writer, somehow, someway. Doing the writing course made me believe in myself even more. I always thought that I would get there in the end but, I wondered, would I still have that belief without the qualification? It didn't do me any harm, that's for sure, and it may have done me a world of good. I think it also made me a bit more professional, polished even. I can't say that it's a must, but it can certainly help. Gets you out in the company of others as well, which is never a bad thing in a lonely writer's life.

I also decided to turn my dissertation for my Master's degree into a book. It is probably my Magnum Opus, a *4000 year history of Israel and Palestine*. I self-published 1000 copies and I managed to sell almost all of them.

Then, I re-staged my original play after a seven-year hiatus. It was good to be back. I subsequently wrote and produced, and sometimes directed, half-a-dozen plays in the next five years, some of them original, and some of them adaptations.

At the same time, I wrote two novels set in the South of France and three works of non-fiction. Two of them went to the top of the Amazon charts in their particular genres.

It was time to make a fuss.

I received the latest edition of *The Writers' and Artists' Yearbook* as a gift from the agent of one of my actors. I contacted every single publisher of non-fiction in the country and told them of my achievement. I got two book publishing deals as a result.

Along the way, I've lived, learned, and laughed, but the one thing that I have also done is write. Always.

So, you want to be a writer? Then you know what you've got to do. Write!

STARTING OUT

Where to begin? Well, at the start, obviously. Every story has a beginning, middle, and end. Start at the beginning.

Let's assume that you have an idea. You've already decided that you want to be a writer. Say your idea is for a book. It may well be that coming-of-age, angst-ridden novel that we all have to get out of our systems. You've read plenty of books, so it's not exactly alien territory. You've just never written one before.

Basically, you're not going to be a writer unless you actually write something down. Let's be honest here. It's unlikely to be a work of genius. It may even be closer to awful. *It doesn't matter.* You're starting out on your journey to be a writer, and every journey begins with a single step. It doesn't matter how small or tentative that step is, it's still a step in the right direction.

Winners have a focus. They set their minds on the goal. In our case, it's to be a writer. So we must begin to write.

You might start with something less ambitious, like a poem or a short story. It doesn't matter. Whatever it is you've decided to write, get it down on paper (or on your computer). Leave it a couple of days, then read it back to yourself. Make any changes that you feel it needs. Now you're editing. The result is your second draft. This is all writing. You're several steps into your journey. Feels good, doesn't it?

Now I'm sure, having decided that you want to be a writer, you've probably already imagined the riches and the amazing life that you're going to lead. It's only natural. There may be a pot of gold at the end of your rainbow. It's fine to think like that. Just don't think that the journey's end is in two steps, or two months, or even in two years' time. It will take as long as it takes.

Similarly, don't be disheartened by the fact that it might take a decade or two (or in my case, three!) before you get your break. You're going to be living your life anyway. This is just something that is going to make you happier along the way.

Make a start. You've found your calling. You have a dream. You're already one of life's lucky people. Better to have a dream than none at all, I think.

Starting out, you're probably going to feel a little all at sea. You won't quite know where you are. You're a stranger in a strange land. You'll need a guide. Well, you have one in your hand right now. You may have a mentor you can call upon, whether that's a teacher or a tutor who believes in you, or your companions at an informal writing group, or even a favourite author who was written a book on writing that has inspired you. It may well be your bible.

Seek support wherever you can find it – as little or as often as you need it – but the reality is that it all comes down to you. To be a writer, you need to write.

When you get to the end of that first completed writing week on your latest project, allow yourself a smile of satisfaction, take a break, and enjoy a weekend off or a night on the town, and then carry on. Get trucking, keep rolling. Output is experience.

Practise, practise, and practise some more. Turn ideas into tangible products such as poems, plays, scripts, and novels.

Michael Owen was a teenage football sensation. He came blessed with God-given talents. Guess what? He still went into training and practiced incredibly hard every day. And by doing so, he improved.

Can writing be taught? Of course it can, but it can only make an average writer out of a mediocre talent. It can also turn a talented writer into a successful one.

But it requires practice. When starting out, you have many, many years of practice ahead of you.

Mark Twain once said, 'Write without pay until someone offers to pay you.' That, effectively, is what is going to happen. He then went on to put a three-year time-line on his advice. I'd definitely discount that last part. If you want to be a writer, you should be in it for the long-haul. For us mere mortals, I think his advice should read, 'Write until someone pays you, however long that takes'.

You can get started by writing for magazines. You can write a review of a gig you've been to, or a play that you've seen, and submit it to your local paper. Don't charge for it. They need content. They might just use it.

Write another good piece, get the name of the arts editor and strike up a rapport, even if it's only via email. Pretty soon, they'll come to expect and to value your input.

They might ask you to review an act that's coming to town. They like your insightful observations and the wit and colour that you put into your reviews. What are you going to say when they ask you? Well, you'll probably reply that you'd love to contribute a piece, however the gig is sold out, or the tickets are £50 each. Can they get you on the guestlist or get you a ticket? Now you're writing reviews. You're writing.

When I was working on the Albert Memorial, we used to venture out as a group about once a month to attend seminars, or visit some interesting city, or a project that had an association with restoration or conservation. One time, we went to explore the various bridges in and around Bristol.

There was a specialist magazine called *Conservation News* who asked my employers if anyone in our group would write an article about our latest trip. My bosses said that they had just the person, and my first-ever published work was an article about the bridges of Bristol for that niche publication.

I then took a girlfriend to a gig one night. She was a fan of Cajun music. There was a guy over from America playing at a venue not too far away. She mentioned that her dad did gig reviews for a Country and Western magazine. She asked me to write a review of the show we'd just seen. She gave it to her father. The result was my second published piece.

A young actor who appeared in a couple of my plays told me how he'd started out in the acting profession. He'd studied drama at university and, upon graduation, applied for every audition that he could find. Some of these were unpaid gigs: students making short films, and the like who needed volunteers and extras.

Several of his peers refused to work for free and dismissed these unpaid gigs out of hand while he volunteered for everything. As well as gaining experience on set, he also earned a lot of goodwill with people who went on to bigger and better things. Low and behold, the paid gigs started to roll in. Meanwhile, many of his fellow acting graduates, who had not been so obliging, were deserting the industry in droves, unable to secure paid work, having neither the experience nor the goodwill in the bank that this other young actor had. I think it's a good example of how to get your break in a creative industry. Art first. Money second. Keep practising.

Remember this: failures are the milestones of success. Your journey must have many milestones; otherwise it's not a journey – it's a stroll. And achieving success in any endeavour is unlikely to resemble a gentle preamble. More than likely, it's going to be an epic journey filled with blood, sweat, and tears. What if a million of us want to be writers, but only 10,000 of us can succeed? It's going to be the ones who put in the effort, the ones who lap up the experience, and the ones who absorb from their peers and their mentors who ultimately win the prize.

The sooner you start, the sooner you'll finish. There are 10,000 hours to go, remember. But keep living. Respect your life and the people in it. And start writing. Put something tangible down on paper. You're a dreamer, not a daydreamer. Get writing.

So, it doesn't matter where you start. It's only important that you do.

FEEDBACK

Everything I've learned, I've learned through feedback. I guess that makes this quite an important chapter. It's a bold statement, but one that I believe. Of course, in order to receive feedback, you first have to write something. That goes without saying.

You write a script, or the first few chapters of a book. You've got something to show someone. The more qualified that person is to judge what you have written, the better the quality of feedback you're going to receive. They don't have to be a professional person, though the more experienced they are, the better it is for you.

If you know someone who likes to read, they'll do perfectly well. If you know someone who likes the movies, they would be a sound reader for your screenplay. Similarly, someone who likes going to the theatre might give you a decent critique of your play.

But, if you are lucky enough to find someone in the actual business – like an actor, an agent, a director, producer, or publisher – then more power to your elbow.

You might say, 'I don't know anyone in the business'. That may be true, but you've heard of the six degrees of separation. You can get to anyone on the planet in six steps, and that includes Steven Spielberg or Stephen King. So, by that rationale, in two or three steps, you should be able to reach someone who has a job in the arts.

I once went out on a Sunday afternoon to watch a game of football at a local pub. I was taking a well-earned break, having been ensconced in my solitary cave, writing a screenplay.

Finishing my drink at the end of the match, I overheard a lively group of people talking at the next table. They were talking about a play they were rehearsing. They were – gasp – a troupe of actors!

I introduced myself as a writer. I asked if anyone would like to read my latest screenplay. I explained that I'd like nothing more than feedback. One of them said they'd be happy to. My first reader found, and feedback soon forthcoming.

We all know people. Do you know someone whose brother or sister or father or mother or cousin or uncle works at a local theatre or in some other corner of the arts? Wrack your brains. I'm sure you do. See? You made the leap in two steps.

Now, you just have to ask them. Fortune favours the brave. If you don't ask, you don't get. And, more importantly, that feedback is crucial to your career. You absolutely need it. So don't be shy. You can't afford to be.

I'll qualify my initial statement above. I've also learned from books, from my Master's degree in Writing, and from the many courses, workshops, and seminars that I've attended. The courses usually involve feedback from your peers anyway, while the books teach you how to create; but it's the feedback to what you create that really shapes you as a writer. Your readers will tell you if you're on the right track, and will hopefully point out the areas where you're going wrong. And there'll be plenty of those to begin with.

It's important to acknowledge that feedback can be good or bad. Your readers will hopefully tell you what bits they liked *and* what bits they didn't. Hopefully, they'll give you reasons why they did or did not like whatever it was that they read.

Remember, if they've been kind enough to take the time to read your work, and the additional time to feedback to you, be gracious when you receive their response. They're doing you the favour, not the other way around, so don't get uppity if they fail to engage with the material or they don't think your hero or your story is the best thing since sliced bread. Try to identify where they disengage with your work. You can correct that flaw next time out. You're improving, thanks to their feedback.

Of course, you don't have to respond to every comment. That way madness lies. If one person loves your main character and your next reader doesn't, how do you accommodate that? The truth is, you can't. Weigh up both opinions and then justify to yourself why your hero acts in a certain way. Ultimately, it's your story. If you can take their opinions on board, maybe hone your character or story accordingly, and still be happy with where you go with it next, then you're a better writer than you were on the previous draft. You're improving, through feedback.

Not everyone responds positively to every story or character. When the movie *Forrest Gump* came out, it seemed that half of the people who saw it loved it, and the other half hated it. A complete division of opinion. And guess what? It didn't matter, because those who loved it and those who hated it still paid the same ten bucks to see it. The producers certainly didn't mind. And it was a water-cooler talking point, which made even more people go and see it – some of whom loved it, and some of whom hated it. But it didn't matter, because those people too paid the same ten bucks.

Don't try to please everyone. It's impossible. Just write the story that you want to tell, and hope that at least *somebody* likes it!

I was lucky that I got someone of the calibre of Alan Rickman to read my first ever script. I still have his handwritten letter. I've also had friends who bumped into actors and pushed my scripts onto them. One friend was a hairdresser. She would always ask her customers, in the way that hairdressers do, 'What do you do?' as she went about the business of cutting their hair. If they responded with anything remotely resembling the arts, she would push me onto them. In this way, she managed to befriend a bloke who was mates with the lead singer of Iron Maiden. Now, my poetry at that time was a world away from anything that one of the world's top heavy-metal bands might have been remotely interested in. It didn't matter. A meeting was set up.

We went to meet Bruce Dickinson in a pub in Chiswick, West London, one evening. There was my friend, Amanda, and myself, plus her customer from the salon and, soon, the long-haired lead singer of Iron Maiden. Bruce explained that he had only popped out for a short while to pick up a takeaway for himself and his wife. He could spare us only five or ten minutes.

He parked his expensive mountain-bike outside as he read through my earnest poems, wondering what on earth he was doing there and what he could possibly do for my fledgling career. Forty-five minutes later, he said his goodbyes, wished me good luck, and went outside, where he discovered his favourite bike had been nicked!

I can't say that the meeting benefited my writing career in any way, but at least we explored the option, and I can now say that I've met the singer of Iron Maiden. Unfortunately for Bruce Dickinson, it's not a night he's likely to forget either!

I'd send scripts and sample chapters of novels out to agents and publishers. Then I'd wait for their responses. You'll know you're making progress when they take the time to offer more than 'Thanks but no thanks', if you're lucky to get even that.

I once wrote a play and, two weeks before the opening night, one of the actors said he needed an opening monologue. It was a Christmas production of *The Tommy Cooper Show* at a small theatre in Liverpool. It was obvious to my very experienced actor that the show should open with a speech. So I sat down and wrote one.

It had to be light-hearted (it was a comedy after all), something Christmassy (if that's even a word!), and it should set the mood for all that was to follow.

So I sat down and wrote a page or two for the actor in question. He would walk out, front and centre, and address the audience before the play properly began.

Two weeks later, on opening night, I sat amongst a packed audience as the actor appeared and delivered his speech. And people laughed. They loved it. It did everything it was supposed to. It relaxed the crowd and put everyone in the mood for the show that they were about to see. And I wrote that! Just two weeks earlier.

It was so fresh that I could still vividly remember sitting down to write it, staring at the blank page, or rather computer screen, letting my thoughts gather, and then starting to type.

Now, here I was, just a fortnight later, hearing the sound of audience-laughter. That's feedback. It told me that I could do this.

That's what feedback does.

Go find it. Got get it. It's important, and you need it.

WRITING COURSES

Is there any point in going on a writing course? Of course there is. I've always thought, and found to be true, that whatever it is that you're trying to learn, you should try to expose yourself to as many different teaching aids as possible. Read a book, do a course, find a mentor, practise by yourself or with others. It's all learning, and by mixing it up, you will gain a much more rounded learning experience.

So, what sort of courses are available, and which of these should you try?

A quick online search will reveal that there are myriad options available. How about a beginner's course in Creative Writing, or a Freelance Journalism course? A Science Fiction and Fantasy course, or even one on how to begin your novel? Most universities now offer a creative writing degree. When I studied for my day job in Quantity Surveying at South Bank University, in London, the sign over the entrance read 'Faculty of the Built Environment'. Within a couple of years, it had followed the then-latest trend and was almost completely taken over by media courses. Everyone, it seems, wants their dream job.

Literary agents are now jumping on the bandwagon and offering courses of their own. The Royal Shakespeare Company even offers a screenwriting course, if you can begin to imagine that.

You can also top up your Bachelor's degree with a Master's, but we're maybe getting a little ahead of ourselves here. Courses can be found anywhere. Locally, you might find a writer's group which will give you a creative outlet and some support for your first endeavours.

I found a beginner's group at my local library when I was first starting out. We'd meet one evening a week, and we'd each take it in turn to read out a short piece of our own writing, and then the rest of the group would pass comment. No one is going to tear you, or your work, to pieces in these sessions. The feedback tends to be towards the supportive end of the spectrum, and at least you're part of a writing community. It will probably spur you on to keep writing so that you have something to read come the next session, or when it's your turn to read next.

When I was going through my film-geek phase in the 1990s, I joined the London Screenwriter's Workshop, in the city where I was living and working at the time. They offered an array of courses, workshops, and seminars, with tutors and speakers who had a track record in the field.

One of the courses was on the subject of 'Breaking the rules'. Screenwriting has quite a rigid structure and, as with anything, you need to know the rules and to have mastered them before you can start to bend and break them.

These courses might last a day or a couple of days over a weekend. There's no particular directive on how long a course should last. Obviously, you're not going to come away with a certificate for completing a one-day course in screenwriting or novel-writing or anything of the sort, but you can still top up your learning by attending a course that is of interest to you.

I once spent a week in France on a writing course, where a published novelist got a freebie holiday for entertaining and educating a group of wannabe writers, including myself. Our number included a literary editor at a major publishing house, an Oxford graduate, a group of hopefuls, and also people who saw writing as a hobby. It was great fun, and it was all learning.

An arts foundation, in the city where I live, would put on regular events including workshops and seminars. I would regularly attend. They'd have guest speakers, and each session would end with a Q&A. Again, a great opportunity to get anything off your chest if you felt you'd hit a wall or a particular stumbling block with your writing. You can also socialise and maybe make contacts that might lead to other opportunities.

Writing can be a lonely occupation. Any excuse to get away from the desk and meet other people – especially like-minded people – is not to be sniffed at, just as long as you're putting in the hours at the writing desk at every other available opportunity.

I'd put it like this. Push yourself as hard as you can to tell the stories that you want to tell, in whatever format best suits the story. When you can't go any further under your own volition, when you've expended every resource available to you at that time, then go seek help. Pick up that 'How-to book', or call your mentor, or go on that course. It will get you over whatever hurdle it is that you're facing.

Then, push yourself as hard as you can, for as long as you can, until you hit the next obstacle that you're absolutely unable to get around or get over. And then find the course or book or person to help you get over that one, and then push yourself for as long and as far as you can until… etc., etc.

Get the picture? Courses are useful. Courses are fun. They don't have to last for four years, or two years, or even one year. They can last a day.

Find the ones that are right for you. Soak up the learning. Don't take the Science Fiction course or the Journalism course unless they're really of use to you (or unless you just want an escape).

Learn what you need to, when you need to.

You can always think about the degree or the Master's degree later on down the line. For now, consider a course of study, involving books and online resources and whatever else you can find. It all goes towards your 10,000 hours.

You want to be a writer, right? Drink from the well of available resources as and when you need to. And then, go write!

WRITING QUALIFICATIONS

What qualifications do you need to be a writer? The answer is none. Or, to be more precise, none whatsoever!

Of course, you need good written English (or whichever language you're writing in), so if you have a certain command of that written language, that can only be a good thing. You could also gain qualifications in a particular subject if that area of expertise is going to be the focus of your writing career.

Ultimately, if you write a play or a screenplay that grabs the attention of an agent, publisher, or producer, they aren't going to question your qualifications. All they will be concerned about is the quality of your work.

In other words, there's nothing stopping you from mastering your chosen art-form and delivering powerful, dramatic writing of your own volition.

I'm not sure Shakespeare ever studied writing in a formal manner. He probably worked out, through trial and error, what worked best for him and his audience. I'm sure he immersed himself in a drama group, lived almost constantly in a theatre-environment, and was a diligent student of his craft and art. And, do you know what, he didn't do half-bad! He became the English language's greatest champion. He did it without qualifications, no letters after his name, but with a passion to share stories and the knowledge of how to drain every ounce of drama from his subject matter and his characters.

And you can do the same.

You won't get a certificate for reading this book, yet it's all part of your learning. The same will be true if you go to a local writing group, or attend a writing seminar, or even jet off to enjoy a novel-writing course in the sun. No certificate, but plenty of experience.

Prior to doing my Master's degree, the only qualification I had was an HND in Quantity Surveying. That didn't stop me turning up to that weekly event at my local library in the company of other amateur writers. It didn't prevent me from securing the post of Script Editor for an award-winning play. It didn't stop me from writing, directing, and producing my own play a couple of years later.

A lack of literary qualifications did not prevent me from having an early screenplay twice optioned. I wrote, I listened to feedback, and I sent my work out speculatively to anyone in the business that I could find.

And as soon as I would finish a script or a book, I'd start another. My output and growing back-catalogue were all the qualifications I needed.

Like I say, write a manuscript that grabs people's attention. That's the only credentials you need. So, if you have the gift of storytelling and the tenacity to sit down and write it, the only thing missing is an audience: either someone to watch it or, in the first instance, someone to read it.

I'm a big fan of non-fiction. Stories seem to have more relevance for me if I know that they are true. Some of the more esteemed non-fiction writers – certainly some of those who top the bestseller charts and seem to garner awards – can boast impressive academic qualifications to support their lofty efforts. They are graduates of some of the world's finest universities. If you were to have such an opportunity, and if you were to take such an opportunity, then it wouldn't do any harm to your future ambitions. In fact, I'm sure it would put you at a distinct advantage.

Most of us will not follow the path of exemplary academic groundwork, yet it is no bar to any of us to go on and achieve our literary aims.

What qualifications do you need to be a writer? Talent and tenacity. That's all you really need. And don't forget to put your work out there, or how else are those movers and shakers ever going to find you?

At my first day at university, albeit studying a different subject to my ultimate goal, our Head of Year gave us this advice.

He said, 'If you were at Oxford or Cambridge right now (we weren't!), people wouldn't ask you what you are studying. They would ask you *what are you reading.*'

Get yourself an education, he advised us. They were going to set us coursework and test us from time to time, but this was an opportunity for every one of us to read around our subject, to spend time in the library, and to get ourselves an education.

I'd like to give the same advice to you. It doesn't matter what qualifications you have, or what letters you have after your name. Get yourself an education.

Read books on writing, attend courses and workshops, join support groups, and maybe take that summer break at a writer's retreat.

You don't need any qualifications to be a writer.

To be a writer, the only qualification is that you write.

PROFESSIONAL ADVICE

I've stated how much faith I have in feedback, so how do you ensure that the feedback you receive is suitably qualified? Well, one way is to pay for it. As I said earlier, utilise your own contacts, or those of friends, family, colleagues, etc., but you can also bolster this by getting some of the real thing.

The thing about professional feedback, or professional anything, is that it comes with a cost. Professionals rarely, if ever, offer their services for free. The clue is in the title. These people are wearing their professional hats at the time that they're working for you. You are their client. As such, they'll expect to be paid.

If you pick up a copy (and you must) of the *Writers' and Artists' Yearbook*, you will find that many of the people in there will state that they won't offer an in-depth commentary on your work. The truth is, most would probably love to, but they just don't have the time. They have so many things occupying their working day that their first loyalty is to their own job and work-load. After all, they need to protect their place in the company hierarchy.

They'll have deadlines and quotas of their own, handed down by their corporate (though, I'm sure, lovely) bosses. You will, unfortunately, be way down their list of priorities. That is, until you write something that they fall in love with, or that gives them pound or dollar signs in their eyes. At that point, they'll engage with you unequivocally. Until then, you may have to fork out some cash to find out if your writing is on the right track or not.

One such service is The Literary Consultancy. I've used it once, and I have no complaints. This was about 20 years ago. I'd written my first attempt at a novel, and I didn't just want to bottom-drawer it upon completion. I wanted to extract every possible benefit from the exercise before moving on to my next book. I paid about £300 for a reader's report. I should imagine that figure has more-or-less doubled by now, as it was a long time ago.

Anyway, in return for that sum, I received a report that was three or four pages long and which highlighted the pros and cons of the work that I had created. They were probably far kinder to me than they needed to be. They were professional and supportive and encouraging. They even said I could call them up to discuss the report if I had any questions. Of course, I took them up on the offer. Extracting every penny, as they say.

They had offered many pointers on how the book could be improved. I phoned the person who had done the report and thanked them for their feedback. I said that I was finished with that story. I was ready to write another. However, if I chose to ignore their advice on how my first book could be improved, would I be missing out on the benefits of trying to make those improvements?

Their response was that it was ultimately my choice, but that they thought it was a good thing when a writer knew when it was time to move on. Sometimes, there is much more to be gained by going on to the next project rather than endlessly raking over the coals of one that was never going to work.

I thought that was fair comment, and it actually liberated me to go on to write my next book.

For many people, working in any branch of the media is actually their dream job. Although there are some who have a 'gate-keeper' quality, most of these people actually love what they do, and love what you do. They'd like nothing more than to give you chapter and verse about your infant screenplay or juvenile play. But they can't. They just don't have the time in their busy working lives.

At the end of the day, it's show-business, and they are involved in the business end of show.

Many of the literary agents and publishers listed in the *Writers' and Artists' Yearbook* now offer to give feedback for a fee. The book also lists numerous other companies offering the same services in a section entitled 'Resources for Writers'.

There are many editors, employed by publishers and literary agents, who freelance as professional report writers offering the in-depth analysis that you want. They'll do it for you in their free time, but you'll have to pay them for the privilege. That's only fair. They're helping with your development. You're paying them to give up their evenings and weekends. Everyone gains.

Beware. There are some editorial services which will do no more than correct your grammar. A comma in the wrong place, here or there, is where they will focus their attention. They might give you a bit of an overall comment on the piece, but that sort of feedback is not going to bring your writing on in leaps and bounds. Better to jump right in and find someone who does this sort of thing for a living, and who wants nothing more than to find an author whose writing will sell in the marketplace.

This is an added bonus of outsourcing your material to a professional. If your stuff is of publishable quality, even if they've read it in their spare time, they will go into work on Monday morning and rave about it. The higher-ups in the department will be told to take a look at it, and they will. It's one way of jumping up a few places in the slush-pile.

What you don't need, at this point, is a proof-reader. You need a story than can grab the attention of readers. If you have to pay for the advice, and if you can afford to do so, then go and do it. It's not a trap, or a rip-off enterprise. It's an area populated by people who love writing and who want to help you. Push yourself as far as you can under your own steam, but seek the help that you need at the time that you need it. Whenever you hit that wall or face that seemingly insurmountable obstacle, grab the resource that gets you over or around it.

You're on a mission, remember. A mission to be a writer. Professionals can help you. Their advice can help you. Choose wisely. Pay what you have to, or whatever you can afford. If not, keep seeking that free support.

You might never need professional help. Maybe your own network can do it for you, or you can work out, for yourself, exactly where you're going wrong and where you can improve. If so, then good for you. But if you suspect that you'll benefit from professional advice, then I say go and get it.

Professional advice is a valuable resource.

THE STORYTELLER'S CRAFT

That's all we are: storytellers. Sometimes, I don't even call myself a writer. I'll just say that I'm a storyteller, or I will think of myself as such. On my gravestone, I'd settle for 'Here lies a storyteller', with hopefully a few more words alongside that!

Writing is how you will communicate the stories that you wish to tell. It is a medium, but the subtext and the theme of what you're actually doing is simply storytelling.

It's an art-form that goes back to the very beginnings of mankind. It pre-dates what we might call civilisation. When we were stone-aged men and women, we would sit around a camp-fire, or in our caves and, at the end of the day, regale ourselves with stories.

These might be stories about the day just spent, or even a mythical narrative about our great forefathers and the beasts of the forests they faced. These stories served to entertain and motivate the tribe, and to engender a shared spirit of community.

There is also, I believe, an in-built story gene in every human being. We, as storytellers, are merely engaging with that host gene every time we begin to tell our tales. Our audience sits transfixed as we offer them the specifics. They cannot help themselves. It's inherent. And, as long as our story hits all of the right marks, our audience is assured.

In fact, I'd go as far as to say that if we ever bore an audience, it is because we have failed to hit those particular marks. It's not the audience's fault. They are sitting there waiting to hear what you have to say. Use this knowledge to hone your own stories to make sure that you leave your audience satisfied, having given them everything that they *want* and *need* to hear.

You may become a playwright, a novelist, or screenwriter. You may bounce between all three or devote your time to one individual arena. Whichever you choose, you will still be telling a story, and storytelling is the DNA that connects the different writing mediums.

I have written several original plays, adapted classic books into plays, written fiction and non-fiction, and also completed a dozen or so feature-length screenplays. They're all stories.

Like any craft, writing needs to be learned. You learn through practice. The beauty of feedback is that it points out where you lost your audience along the way or where you failed to engage them sufficiently. You know it's not their fault (as it's in their DNA), so how can you polish your story to leave only the highlights that push all the right buttons?

My first attempt at a novel was a ponderous affair. My God, how I must have bored the small audience that I found to read it. Talk about going around the houses. I waffled, and waffled, and then waffled some more.

I was over-thinking it. Explaining too hard and too much. Every iota of action was drenched in an avalanche of superfluous words. I didn't stick to the point or get to the heart of the story.

Now here's a thing. Baby crocodiles, upon hatching, identify the first thing that they set eyes upon as their mother. I don't know how long it takes them to shake that notion, should anything other than its real mother be in the vicinity, but the point is, that first response is ingrained in their DNA.

The same is true of your audience. As soon as you start to tell an engaging story, nothing else seems to matter. They are compelled to listen. Well, you'd be a fool (or just an inexperienced writer) to then let their attention wane. You owe it to them to keep them rapt. They are under your hypnotic storytelling spell, and it is your duty as a writer to keep them there.

Any craftsman has to put in the hours to learn their trade. They have to practise and hone their skills. The tools of your storytelling trade are the words that you write. So keep writing, but never forget that what you are really doing is telling stories.

You are a standard-bearer for an ancient tradition. Some are warriors, some are leaders, some are cannon-fodder. All have their part to play. Your role is one that was revered by the first communities in which they lived. Like a tribal witch-doctor, you have the power to lift the spirits of your tribe, to strike fear or to banish it, through the tales that you tell. You can entertain and educate, and afford people a release from whatever thoughts or troubles they hold at the time. You can take over, for a short time, and hold their attention and transport them through your narrative to another time and place.

What stories engage you? You may lean towards a particular genre, such as crime or horror or comedy. This will provide a framework for your story, but you must also be passionate about the story that you wish to tell.

If you're writing for an hour or more at the end of a hard day's work, or at the weekend when there's a free music festival taking place just up the road, then why on earth would you give up your precious time to tell a story that you weren't desperate to share with the world?

Find your passion, tell your story, write your book, play, or film script. And never forget that – first and foremost – you're a storyteller. Your audience awaits and expects you to deliver.

I was in a bookstore one time. I picked up a random novel that caught my eye and turned it over to read the blurb on the back. I noticed that one of the reviews was by two-time Pulitzer Prize-winning author Norman Mailer, a real heavyweight of the writing world. How had a first-time novelist attracted comment from such an esteemed man of letters? The review praised the content of the book, and then Mailer confessed that the author was actually his son-in-law. But, he added, he would have still said the same thing about the book had its author been no relation at all, because, he said, 'Literature is thicker than blood!'

It was a great quote from a great writer. I'd first discovered Mailer when I'd picked up a copy of his book *The Executioner's Song* many years before. I opened up the first page and read the opening paragraph. I knew instinctively that this was a book I wanted to read, just by reading the first few lines.

You probably do the same thing when choosing a book. You open the first page and read a couple of paragraphs and you know, there and then, whether it's something you want to keep reading. How? Well, all writers have a voice, and you will know if that particular voice appeals to you. Most importantly, you will know straight away if that storyteller has grabbed your attention, and if you simply have to stop everything that you're doing to listen to that person tell you a story.

That's the storyteller's art. That's what you need to do.

So remember, you're not just a writer. You're a storyteller.

JOSEPH CAMPBELL

Joseph Campbell defined the art of storytelling in his best-selling book *Hero with a Thousand Faces*. In this seminal work, considered a classic of the genre, Campbell outlined the use of myth and the archetypes that exist in every single story.

I've stated that we have an in-built story gene that makes us a ready-made audience for a well-told story. Joseph Campbell identified the various stage-posts along the way for your story to hit the mark.

Added to this, he further identified the people who should populate that story, outlining the hero's journey and the various characters that he or she was likely to meet along the way.

Fascinating stuff.

There are only said to be five different stories anyway, and every single story ever told will, at its heart, really be a resemblance or a variation of these five ideas.

They are, and I quote:

1. Overcoming the monster
2. Voyage and return
3. From rags to riches
4. A quest
5. Rebirth

These five basic story ideas are then said to fall into a further category of either comedy or tragedy.

On the face of it, just ten categories might be seen to stymie creativity, but within those two settings (comedy and tragedy), and the five different story types, there is a world of opportunities to blend, cross-over, re-invent, move between, subvert, and re-imagine.

What Joseph Campbell did was to identify the subtext to a winning story. He pointed out that all myths, even those that emerged on different continents and in different periods of history, still followed an identifiable pattern.

Whoever we see early on in our story, whoever we first get a feel for, they will be our hero, and it is their story that we will engage with and follow. The hero will then receive a call to adventure. The hero will, at first, refuse to answer that call. After all, they can't be seen to be reckless. We all have day jobs and responsibilities. Who on earth would identify with someone who abandoned everything at the first hint of adventure?

There will then be an inciting incident that causes the hero to change their mind and set out on the quest after all. This can't be done with careless abandon. Events must have transpired that have caused them to act.

Campbell calls this eventual response, 'Crossing the first threshold'.

The hero then enters the belly of the whale.

By this, I think he means that he is inside a situation that he has little or no control over. He's involved in something bigger than himself. The inside of the whale is now his new landscape and environment. He obviously can't stay there forever, and he will need to use all of his (or her) ingenuity to overcome the many obstacles that they will face in order to escape.

He is now on, what Campbell calls, 'The road of trials'.

The hero will meet friends and foes along the way. These people may possess special powers that may help or hinder him.

The hero will have a goal. Ultimately, he will (in all likelihood) achieve that goal, and then he will be able to begin the road back. But, at first, he will refuse to return. Maybe something is keeping him there, like a love interest, or the fate of the locals who will then be left behind and who may be imperilled without his valour to protect them.

Eventually, he will have satisfied the conditions that allow him to return with the cherished prize, and with his conscience and the fair-maiden saved too.

He crosses the return threshold. He is now Master of the Two Worlds, for he has conquered the strange land, and he can also take all of that newfound glory, wealth, knowledge, or whatever it is that he's won, back into his original environment.

He is the same person, except that he's changed in some fundamental way. His ultimate reward is the freedom to live as he wants because he's overcome all of the challenges and conquered all of his fears.

Joseph Campbell expertly explained this in his book, and it has proven to be one of the most inspirational and enduring works on the subject of storytelling.

When you come to write stories of your own, I believe you should write from the heart, with a particular passion for your subject. You can then ask yourself if, when, and how your story correlates to the ancient storytelling art.

You have to grab your readers and hold their attention, in exactly the same way as if you were telling a story around a campfire, ancient or otherwise. Can you do that? You must.

That is your job as a writer. Joseph Campbell's work may add an extra psychological layer to your work. You should check it out anyway, and tick it off your 10,000 hours.

You follow an ancient tradition. You're a storyteller. And your audience awaits.

HOW TO WRITE A PLAY

Enough prevaricating, I hear you say. Yes, we want to be writers. We understand our place in the cosmos and in posterity. Now, just tell us how to do it!

David Mamet is an esteemed playwright who has directed feature film versions of several of his own plays. Yet he had no experience of film directing. He could only do what felt right for him. If it felt right, it was right. That was how he got through it. And that, I believe, is the way to go about writing your own plays. Do it your own way.

There is a format to follow in terms of layout. Essentially, the actors – especially experienced actors – will expect your play to have a certain look. There are several ways that you can achieve this; as long as you separate the description and scene-setting from the actual dialogue, you will end up with a workable script. Ultimately, actors (at least the humble ones) often quote that their job is simply to remember their lines and not bump into the furniture!

One of your jobs is to separate that furniture from the actors' lines in your script. It's just a question of layout. Go to the BBC Writers Room website and search for sample scripts. You'll instantly see how a script should be laid out. A script for radio, theatre, television, or film, will not vary too much in terms of layout. Separate the descriptions, e.g., living room, bar, bedroom, etc. from the dialogue and you're not going to go too far wrong.

So, how do you write a play? Well, you need an idea, first and foremost, one that you are desperate to share with the world.

In my case, I read a book that I found in a library. It was non-fiction, about the murder of John Lennon, alleging that it was a CIA conspiracy, and essentially a politically-motivated assassination. Immediately, I felt that it would work on the stage. I had the requisite passion for the story, yet I had no idea how to turn it into a play. I had no idea even how to write a play. This was still very early on in my writing career, or very soon after I'd realised that I wanted to be a writer.

Eventually, having worked as a Script Editor on someone else's play (and that play having won an award), and also having a few more years writing experience under my belt, I felt ready to tackle the story.

So, you decide which characters you need to tell that particular story. Each character will need to be played by an actor, and unless you've got an 'in' at the National Theatre, you probably want to keep numbers down to a manageable handful.

It's not worth finding an actor just to give them one line in your play, even if that line delivers a vital piece of information. You're going to have to give that line to another actor. You have to use artistic license. Get creative.

You have a story idea with a beginning, middle and end; you have a setting for that story, and you have characters who will live and breathe that story for the time that it's on stage. Those are your parameters.

In the case of my first play, I needed a John and Yoko, a Mark Chapman, and three characters portraying the conspiracy side of the story. The first of these characters was a Rambo-type Vietnam vet who befriends John Lennon's killer and who unwittingly leads him into the clutches of the CIA's dirty-tricks department. The second was the head of operations (the man ultimately pulling the strings), and the third was a hurdy-gurdy head doctor who effectively brainwashes Mark Chapman to carry out the assassination.

So, you now have a cast of characters and a story. What happens next? Well, you do some research. What is happening in the world at the time of your story? Does any of that have relevance to your plot?

Give yourself the time and space to think about your story. Explore every angle. Who are the characters? What do they want? Are there any specific bits of dialogue you want to include, or points that you want to make?

I personally like to jot down notes of things that I want the play to say. Anything that comes to mind that you think has relevance and you wish to include; put it in your writing journal. It may take a month or two of free-thinking before you feel ready, in fact are itching, to move on to the next stage.

Then, you can make a list, a scene-by-scene running order for maybe a two-act play.

Read through it. How does it look on the page? Does it flow? Is there energy and entertainment and variety as you move from the opening scene to the ultimate finale?

Once you have an order of scenes, a roadmap for the play, you're ready to begin writing. You write the words 'Act One. Scene One'. You describe the setting. Then, your characters begin to speak. These characters might be based on real people, or they can be conjured solely from your imagination.

You'll want all of your characters to play a big part, otherwise how is it going to appeal to actors of the calibre that you want to attract. You are the puppet-master, the omniscient creator. This is your time to have fun and feel empowered, because you are the master of the universe that you're about to create.

Tell the story that you want to tell. Include all of the information, all of the nuance, all of the comedy, tragedy, music, and anything else that you have to share.

Make your dialogue interesting. This is your chance to shine as a writer. Can I say this line somehow differently? Don't go for the obvious. Can you make it funnier, more poignant, more meaty?

Do your scenes inspire or unsettle? Do they sparkle with electricity? Will your audience be on the edge of their seats as they wait to see what happens next? This is the challenge you must set yourself and that you must meet as a writer. Have you written a great play, or simply an adequate one? If it's the latter, can you make your story stronger, your characters more memorable, your dialogue more piquant?

Imagine if your play gets produced. There will (hopefully) be an audience to appreciate it and who will judge you on your efforts. How long does your play last? One hour? Two hours? Three (God forbid!)?

Imagine yourself as a storyteller again, just for an instant.

In the oral tradition, if you were talking to someone for an hour – even if you had their undivided attention – would you continue with a monotone story for the whole of that time?

Of course you wouldn't. Your listener would grow bored. You have to mix it up a bit. Show them something exciting, and then maybe take it down a level or two in order to allow them to recuperate. Explore other aspects of the story or fill in the background.

Then they need shaking up again. You move back to high drama. You tell them a joke because they've not laughed for a while. Then, when they settle back into the more prosaic elements of the story, you burst into song or introduce a sudden burst of gunfire.

Keep your audience on their toes. And never let them get ahead of you by guessing what's coming next.

Give your actors a script that allows them to tell the story that you wish to tell, in a way that audiences want to hear.

That's how you write a play.

Noel Coward, the iconic British playwright, claimed that it was possible to write a play in a weekend. He said he'd done just that when he wrote *Blithe Spirit*, which he created while staying at a hotel overlooking the sea in the quaint, eccentric faux-Italian village of Portmeirion in Wales.

Coward also once stated that you could do anything to a theatre audience. He said that you can coax them, charm them, shock them, scare them, make them laugh, make them cry, but the one thing that you should *never ever do* is bore them.

Remember that one. It's the perfect piece of advice.

THE PLAYWRIGHT AS PRODUCER

How do you get your play onto the stage? Well, you could always produce it yourself. I have produced nearly all of my own plays, except for one that has run off without me!

Now, there is a theory that there are none-so-mad as the self-produced, and there is certainly some truth in that. However, if you believe in what you have created, why not try it out in front of an audience? This could be something as simple as a rehearsed reading with a group of actors, or a night or two at your local community centre, or upstairs in your local pub.

There are small theatres or venues in every town, village, and city in the world that can be hired for a small fee or are even available free of charge (though the latter is quite rare). These smaller venues serve as stepping stones to larger stages. They are approachable and, in fact, are usually crying out for you to hire them.

When I wrote my first play, I already knew some of the actors that I wanted to use. Indeed, I had written the play with some of them in mind as they were friends and I had worked with them before.

I could hear the words being spoken. I knew how good it could all be. So, when all I heard was warm (ish) praise for the script, I thought I'd grab the bull by the horns and hire a local theatre and put the play on myself.

What did I need? Well, the script, obviously. After that, I needed to cast all of the parts. There were six actors in my play. Two of them I already knew. The rest I found through sites such as Casting Call Pro on the internet. One guy I spotted on the television soap *Emmerdale*, and I then bumped into him as he worked as a bouncer at my local nightclub. You can't write this stuff!

By now, I had a script and a cast. I booked a short run of three evening performances at a theatre which housed 150 people. I now had a venue to go with my script and cast.

I needed to publicise the show, so I gave the theatre an eye-catching image and a bit of text for their quarterly magazine that advertised forthcoming productions.

I didn't get any flyers or posters done, and paid for this with poor ticket-sales for the first couple of shows. Luckily, word of mouth came to my rescue, and we achieved a sell-out audience for the last night of the run. In my defence, it *was* my first production. You're bound to make mistakes first time out.

Once I had the script, the cast, and the venue, I needed to find a rehearsal space. I also needed a set, some costumes, and a few props. Soon, I had a venue, a group of (very good) actors, a set, costumes, and a script. I was ready to go. The whole thing took nine months from blank page to full house. And, by seeing my work in front of an audience, I felt like I'd put myself through the best drama and writing course ever.

I probably lost five grand on the play, a blow which would have been softened had I better advertised those first couple of nights. However, if I'd packed my job in for a year to go on a writing course, I'd probably have foregone five times that amount in lost wages. So, it wasn't bad value for money, in terms of what I gained in experience as a writer. Plus, it was a hell of a laugh. Best time of my life, possibly.

I've since gone on to produce spectaculars such as *Frankenstein* at Liverpool's Bombed Out Church on Halloween. That was a good one. Even my wife was impressed! Other plays of mine have played the Grand in Blackpool and many of the finest theatres in the land, plus many of the small stepping stone theatres as well.

Don't be afraid to produce your own work, as long as you know at least something about what you're doing. Don't be afraid to start small. It's the best place for all of us budding writers, actors, directors, and producers.

If it goes well, and if you've enjoyed the experience, then why not do it again? As long as it's not costing you money, or at least not too much, I'd say there is a lot to gain from seeing your work produced, even if you have to step into the role of producer yourself. You never know, you may even make some money at it, although please don't take that as a given.

Even if the play is a cracker, you may still end up footing the bill for it. It's not for the fickle or the fainthearted, but at least you can say that you've seen your work on stage.

And you never know who might be in the audience. I've had winners of Oscars and Tony Awards see my work. They may have a friend or a cousin in the cast. They show up to support them, yet it's your work that they're listening to and watching. Someone of influence may then spot your talent. How are they going to do that if all of your work ends up in the bottom drawer of your writing desk at home?

I know a lady who took some of her work to the Edinburgh Fringe Festival, which is a great place to go and either watch plays or showcase your writing. She's now a (well-paid) writer on *Coronation Street*.

Another example of your own producing power is when it comes to the writing itself. If you create a piece that calls for thousands of extras or a huge amount of equipment, then who on earth is going to fund all that? You can exercise self-control at the writing stage so that, if a producer does feel passionately about your work, they won't be put off by the inherent costs of putting it in front of an audience.

Maybe you combine characters so that you (or another producer) are only paying one actor's wages instead of two? I once did a production of *Great Expectations* at the Grand Central Hall in Liverpool and at the Shelley Theatre in Bournemouth. It was my own adaptation. Most of the cast were pulled from my own pool of actors; people I'd worked with (sometimes several times) before.

There was the character of Pip's Uncle Pumblechook and the character of the lawyer, Mr Jaggers. Both were of similar age. One has prominence in the first half of the story, the other comes to the fore in the second half. Why put an actor on stage for half the show, only for another actor to appear after the interval?

I combined the two characters, gave the individual actor a much better part to play, and saved myself on wages, accommodation, and travel, etc. *I was writing with my producer's hat on.*

You can do the same. And this doesn't just apply to playwriting. You can apply it to all of your writing, especially screenwriting. Someone is going to have to stump up for those production costs. After all, we should hope to see a profit for all of our hard work. If you can cut your cloth at certain moments, you will increase the attractiveness of your script for a budget-conscious producer.

I notice that Amazon (and many other outlets) are now producing their own original films and TV series. One of the first films Amazon produced was an Afghanistan-set war film (*The Wall*), which featured a cast of just three or four individuals stuck in an extreme and tense situation. What are the chances that someone read that script and thought, 'Great story, and also cheap to produce'. I'd say the chances are quite high.

So, write with passion, tell the story that you want to tell, but be mindful that if you write the world's most expensive screenplay or play, you are limiting your chances of seeing it on stage or on the big screen.

Aim to be the best, but aim to be produced, either by yourself or by someone else. Otherwise, you're just a writer in the dark.

HOW TO ADAPT A PLAY

The first play that I wrote was adapted from a book. The book was essentially non-fiction, written by a legal journalist, and so it seemed like the source-material was merely the research that I based the play on, rather than a literary adaptation. Of course, I needed permission from the book's author.

A quick look at the first couple of pages and I found the publisher's name and address. I wrote and told them of my wish to turn the book into a play. After some discussion, permission was granted, and I wrote an original play based on someone else's research.

My first proper adaptation came when I did *Frankenstein* and, at this point, I'd written and produced four original plays of my own. I felt ready to tackle a real adaptation.

Why did I even bother? Why not just write another original play? Well, my four previous plays were stories that I was just dying to tell. I had that innate passion. I had ideas for stories that I was desperate to share with the world. I had no other option but to create original pieces of writing with which to tell those stories.

In the case of my first real adaptation, I had spotted a young actor on stage that I really wanted to work with. I thought he was unique. His voice was incredible. The nuance and inflection and authority of his voice reminded me – I kid you not – of Sir Anthony Hopkins. I thought, 'this kid deserves to be heard'.

At the time, there was no story that I had a pressing need to create, so I began to think about what books existed already that I could adapt.

I'd spotted the young actor in a student performance of Oscar Wilde's *Dorian Gray*. The actor seemed well-suited to a period piece. This also meant that I could find a book that was possibly out of copyright. I could therefore set about an adaptation without the need to get involved in negotiations for the performance rights.

I looked along my own bookshelf. I may as well choose a book that I'd read and hopefully loved. I found *Frankenstein*, Mary Shelley's masterpiece. It was, and remains to this day, one of my three favourite books of all time. The part of Doctor Frankenstein, that madman / genius, would be a perfect fit for our young actor, who had his own wild mop of hair.

I knew that I would only consider a cast of five or six actors. The same had been true for all of my previous plays. I re-read the book to find out which of the supporting characters should play a part in my dramatic reconstruction.

Obviously, there's got to be The Monster: a hell of a part. Then, there's Frankenstein's love-interest, Elizabeth. She should also have a friend in whom to confide, and who better but the part of Justine, who goes innocently to the gallows after the monster commits one of his despicable crimes and then frames the poor girl.

Victor Frankenstein, too, should have a friend, for which we have the dashing Henry Clerval. Finally, I chose to include Professor Waldman, who teaches Victor about science and chemistry at the University of Geneva, unwittingly drawing out the skills that he will need to discover the mystery of life itself.

What, I hear you say? Is there no place for Mr Frankenstein the elder, who introduces young Elizabeth into their household? Is there no place for the young boy whose murder is the first that The Monster commits? Or what about the blind man who teaches the creature to speak, not realising the wretchedness of his pupil? And what about a whole posse of villagers to chase the monster from their midst?

Well, I had no time, space, or money for any of them, I'm afraid. I had to make do with what I could afford. I had to get creative. My cast of six would have to carry the entire story.

And which scenes to include? Well, rather than damage my own treasured copy of the book, I bought a new cheaper version, which I proceeded to read, using a highlighter pen to mark any scenes I thought were suitable for inclusion.

So, I had a cast of characters and a list of scenes to include.

I started to plot the action, act by act, scene by scene. I thought it should be a story told in two short acts, each about 30 to 40 minutes long, with a 15-minute interval in between. We'd be all done and dusted within an hour and a half at the very most. And that included the interval. Short and sweet.

I hate those plays that last three hours. There is some justification for your big West End musicals, at £150 a ticket, to give you your money's worth, but there is rarely any justification for almost any other play to last as long. Most of it is art for art's sake, as fake as the Emperor's new clothes, and is one of the reasons that theatre is not universally loved. It is to the detriment of the medium that some people like to show how clever they are by keeping you there for half the night.

Even if you love the first hour of a play, by the end of the second hour, you're there on sufferance. And, by the end of the third hour, you're ready to kill everyone in the room! So, bring people in, tell them a story, and then let them go and enjoy the rest of the evening with the friends that they came with.

They'll love you for it. Trust me!

First act, introduce your characters, set up the premise of the story (in this case, a restless young man with a thirst for knowledge), create some emotional ballast (the blossoming love between Victor and Elizabeth), and get the audience to know the supporting characters (Justine and Henry) so that they feel something for them when their own stories and sorry endings come to the fore later on.

Show Victor getting lost in his studies. Show his single-minded focus to go where no man has ever been before, as he challenges the Gods in order to create life out of nothing.

He finally finishes his brutal work and forms the creature. As the thunder roars and the lightning crackles all around him, the yellow eye of the monster, laid out on the slab before him, slowly opens. And Victor Frankenstein stands over his creation and screams to the heavens: "Life!"

End of Act One.

Time for a beer and a trip to the loo.

The second act sees the monster abandoned by his creator, who has finally come to his senses now that his terrible work is complete. The monster is lost and alone in the world. Misery makes him a fiend. He acts out his vengeance, set squarely on the man who made him and then tossed him aside.

Remember this: *in your writing, always keep moving, and always aim for the end.* That's a tip from top playwright and screenwriter Budd Schulberg (*On The Waterfront*). Again, you don't want to bore your audience. Ever.

The play moves swiftly towards its denouement. That's the bit where all the various strands come together, just before the ultimate completion and end of the tale. There's loads to fit in. The monster challenging Victor to make him a female monster, so that they may go off together and never meet with or menace mankind again.

Victor sets about the task, but he wonders what might happen if they were to breed. He can't finish the job, and dashes his latest creation to pieces.

When the monster turns up to collect his other half, how is Victor going to tell him that he's smashed her to smithereens? Would you tell him? I bloody wouldn't!

So what of Victor's own forthcoming wedding to Elizabeth? How's that night now going to go?

The answer, of course, is badly.

That was the play. That was my theatrical adaptation of *Frankenstein*.

We organised a fair amount of publicity for an event that sold out three weeks in advance. Unsurprising really. It was a great idea, played out on Halloween, at a unique and much-loved venue (for which I have to give credit to my wife, Lesley, whose idea it was to stage it there).

We had a local TV station come in to record some of the rehearsals and do a few interviews with myself and the cast. The interviewer asked me which version of *Frankenstein* I was doing. Was I doing the National Theatre's version, complete with 49 different scenes and about the same number of actors?

No, I was not, I replied. I would never have done their version for a number of reasons. Firstly, I was a small, independent producer. I could never have afforded to stage such an extravaganza. But, also, I wouldn't have wanted to. I knew my audience. They wanted short (ish) and sweet. It had never let me down before. Why change something that you know works for you?

Most of all, it had never even occurred to me to see what other theatrical versions of the story existed. I wanted to do it my way. Never mind the fact I'd have had to acquire the rights and pay royalties for the National Theatre's version; I wanted to tell the story of one of my favourite books with the same passion that I felt when writing my earlier original plays.

I read recently, in an interview with a successful screenwriter, that if you write with a passion for your subject – whether or not that project is ultimately successful – it will still be some of your best writing. When you write *without* passion for your subject, it will really be some of your worst.

I'd say that whenever you adapt a work for the stage, find your passion for the story, tell it the way you want to, and never lose sight of what works for you.

At the end of the day, it will still have your name on it, you will still be judged by it, and if you're trying to make a name for yourself, it had better be good.

Treat an adaptation no differently to how you would craft one of your own original creations. You've got both the help and the hindrance of someone having had the idea before you, and having delivered it in its original form, but the adaptation is all yours.

Go forth, deliver, enjoy, and *never ever bore.*

FROM WHERE COMES INSPIRATION?

Is this the million-dollar question? If you can pinpoint where to find inspiration, well, all you have to do then is sit yourself down and type the thing up, and you've got it made. Right? Well, maybe. As Thomas Edison once famously said, "Genius is one percent inspiration and ninety-nine percent perspiration". But where, exactly, does inspiration come from?

Well, we're all different, but I guess some thinking-time helps. You might get yours while out fishing, or walking the dog, or just walking through your local park.

You might stare out the window at home, or maybe you have your best ideas while sitting on the loo. Maybe you go and grab a coffee at your favourite cafeteria.

Wherever it is, I'm sure that having a place where you can be alone with your thoughts is a good place to come up with an idea for a story.

Mary Shelley came up with the idea for *Frankenstein* when she was travelling around Europe with her husband, the poet Percy Shelley, and their good friend Lord Byron (yes, the guy who was mad, bad, and dangerous to know). So, she was a creative person anyway, surrounded by equally creative people.

They were staying in a cabin in the woods, and one night they came across a book of German ghost stories, which they would read to each other around the log fire at night. You're getting the picture, almost an *ideal* setting for the subconscious to get to work.

They challenged each other to see who could come up with a good idea for a ghost story.

One night, Mary dreamt about a creature being formed from body parts that suddenly sprung to life. She had created life where it should not have existed. She was so startled by the dream that she actually woke up in a cold sweat.

The next night, when asked if anyone had thought up a good ghost story, Mary said that she had. And thus was the genesis of the Frankenstein phenomenon.

Stephen King, in his book *On Writing* said that he got the idea for his first published novel, *Carrie*, from two different sources. The first was while working at a school and being asked to clean the girls' locker room. He and a co-worker entered the room after school hours. It was unlike any boys' locker room he'd ever been in. It was, frankly, another world.

An insight into the lives of teenage girls. The showers had privacy cubicles. There were vending machines on the wall that served the needs of female adolescents.

He'd previously read an article in a magazine about telekinesis and the power of poltergeists. He'd read that these powers were particularly powerful in young girls, especially around the time of their first period.

He started to imagine a naïve teenager having her first period in the shower at school and not knowing what it was. The other girls are being mean to her. How does she fight back? Well, by using her powers of telekinesis, of course.

The idea for *Carrie* was born.

One night, I walked into my local pub and found my friend talking to a man who was writing an article for a magazine. The article was going to be about the pub itself, which had been there for 150 years and had a certain amount of character.

'Tell me something interesting about this pub', the journalist said to me.

'Well', I replied, 'Adolf Hitler used to drink here'.

He was shocked. I looked (at least I hoped I did) sane. How could I come out with such a ludicrous statement? I explained.

'Adolf Hitler's brother, Alois, lived 150 yards in that direction', I said, pointing. (That's 100 percent fact.) There is a German church 150 yards in the opposite direction. (Also 100 percent fact.) According to Alois's wife's memoirs, Adolf came to stay with them for six months from November 1912 to April 1913 (that's 100 percent fact, according to her book).

'So', I said, 'don't tell me that he didn't call into this pub and have a quick half on his way home from church!'

A few months later, I was in that same pub when I picked up a copy of the magazine, in which the journalist had quoted me word for word, albeit with some incredulity.

I thought, 'I absolutely believe that story'. I was convinced that Adolf Hitler had stayed in my home city of Liverpool 100 years earlier. Then, I thought, I wonder what he did for those six months. Wow! Was that a light-bulb moment or what?

I knew immediately that I had a great idea for a play.

Hitler would come to Liverpool (and why does he come?).

He would hang around for six months (and what did he do all day?).

Then he would go back (why does he leave?).

They would be the questions I would ask myself, and that I would hopefully answer.

The play became *Adolf in Toxteth*. It was performed at the Actor's Studio in Liverpool in 2012, the Unity Theatre in the same city in 2016, and I'm still not done with it yet.

My next play came about when I visited a local tourist attraction, The Williamson Tunnels. In 2019, the venue won the Liverpool Tourist industry award for Best Visitor attraction. Back in 2013, I wrote a play about the life of the extraordinary man who built a vast network of tunnels under the city. The reason these tunnels were ever built remains a mystery to the present day; however, I had my own idea as to why…

So, the play was inspired by a man who was an inspiration to me. Inspiration can simply be that: the act of being inspired by someone or something.

I once spent three months in the South of France. While I was there, I expected to do nothing more than learn a little French, and do a spot of writing. Little did I know that the place where I stayed had such a rich history or, that when I came back, the town would become the inspiration for two novels. Both are now available on Amazon under the titles *Freetown* and *The Girl Who Disappeared*.

Inspiration can, therefore, be a place.

When we were rehearsing my play *One Bad Thing – the Murder of John Lennon*, the actor playing Lennon was messing around one day during rehearsals doing impressions of Tommy Cooper.

It inspired me to create a play for him about the legendary comedian / magician, and I later got a book deal on the back of the play to write my own Cooper biography.

A deadline might also give you inspiration. If you're struggling to find something to write about, but you've got a contract to fulfil or a deadline to meet, I bet you'll rack your brains until you come up with something. Anything.

If you ever find yourself wondering 'What if?' That's a hell of a great starting point. It usually means that you're the first person to think of that idea. *Jaws*, the movie, came about when the writer John Bentley asked himself, 'What if a Great White Shark suddenly grew territorial?' It would obviously terrorize whatever community it latched itself on to. What if? It's usually a thought worthy of further creative exploration.

A recent movie, entitled *Yesterday*, has a similar 'what if' premise. What if someone woke up one day and found out that they were the only person alive who remembered the music of The Beatles?

If you're lucky enough to have a 'what if?' moment, try and see if you can develop it into an outline for a story, and then flesh it out further into a play, a script, or a book. Like I say, it usually means that you're the first person to have had that idea. Cherish it and embellish it.

Charles Dickens, no doubt, found inspiration in the characters and the poverty that he saw all around him in the England of his era. Can you draw inspiration from your own age and your own circumstances?

They say 'write what you know'. What do you know?

There are books available on Amazon that offer tips and exercises to get your creative juices flowing. Maybe check one of them out. It won't do you any harm.

They say the best cure for writer's block is to get a day job. If you're itching to get to your story, the preceding eight or ten hours of reality will focus your mind.

What you write – when you get there – is whatever story you feel compelled to share with the world. That inspiration could have come from anywhere, but you probably know the type of tale you like to tell, or the genre that you want to work in.

When I wrote my book on Israel and Palestine, I spent 18 months researching the subject before I spent a further year writing, editing, and publishing my work.

There was a particular point during my research and writing when I stumbled on a hypothesis that more-or-less shook me to the core. Call it a revelation. I thought I'd discovered a previously untold theory regarding the Exodus of the Israelites out of Egypt. I then covered it briefly in my book, but I knew that I wanted to examine it in much greater detail.

I went back to it later on, and wrote and published it as *The Pharaoh Moses*. It's a book of which I'm very proud. I think my passion and enthusiasm for the theory stands out in the writing. So, inspiration can even crop up while you're busy writing something else.

Ultimately, I think it's true to say that inspiration can come from anywhere. It can come from a person or a place, or it can come about by the simple fact that you're a creative person searching for a story to write or tell.

Afford yourself the time to think, and find your special place or places in which to nurture those creative thoughts (three months in the South of France is a pretty good one!).

You're going to need that inspiration, and those 'what if' moments in order to stay ahead of the pack, or even to be a minor part of it.

What inspires you? Your ambition to be a writer, that's what. So go and find it.

GET YOURSELF ON A SHELF

Now, obviously, the shelf that we all want to be on is the one in our local bookstore, library, or at one of the national bookselling chains. In this era of eBooks and online purchasing, that's no longer as important as it once was, but it's still great if you can get there.

What I'm actually talking about is getting yourself on a shelf while you're in the middle of the writing phase, so that you don't lose the flow when real life gets in the way of your writing.

Say you've started a novel, but you have a big family holiday planned. You don't want your work to grind to a halt after three months of endeavour, returning after a break thinking, 'how do I pick up the thread of this?' How can I rediscover that energy and passion?

Because, once you start writing, at times you'll be fairly flying. You'll have smoke coming off the keyboard as your fingers race to keep up with the thoughts pouring into and out of your mind.

And then it stops. The cab's outside. All of your family are dressed in their finest to attend that family wedding, or the suitcases are stacked by the door ready to take that week or fortnight-long vacation.

You don't want to go. Or, at least, you'd love to go and still be able to hold that thought and pick up at the same pace, and in the same place, as soon as you get back. So how do you do that? You get yourself on a shelf.

I think of it like rock-climbing.

You wouldn't decide to take a break while you were dangling from a rope halfway up, would you? You'd want to get yourself onto a ledge before taking that well-earned breather. The same with your writing.

If you know that something is coming up on the horizon that is going to interfere with your writing programme, aim to get *to the end* of a chapter, section, or an act of your play or screenplay, and then you can go off and enjoy yourself knowing that you're at a natural break in proceedings.

There are two schools of thought as to how you should end your own writing day. I'm assuming that you're serious about this whole endeavour, and that you will be putting pen to paper, or fingers to keyboard, and creating something at some point. Assuming I'm correct about that, I'd like to think that you're going to try and write every day, or almost every day. Even if you set yourself a weekly target of 1,000 or 10,000 words, you might not need to write every day, but you still need to hit your target each week.

How do you keep that up?

Well, I have heard it said, and I can't dispute it, that you may want to leave a sentence up in the air at the end of your writing session, and that way you can just jump back into it.

Personally speaking, I like to complete each section before I break for the day.

Take this book, for example. The one that you're reading right now. I aim to write a chapter every day or night.

There are about 50 chapters in this book. Each contains about 1,000 words. That's my target every time that I sit down to write.

After a couple of months of writing, plus another month to let it settle and to afford myself the space and time to edit, I'll have written a new book.

If I'm lucky enough to get a publisher on board for it, there might then be another month or two bat-and-balling it between ourselves to get it up to the required standard and in the fashion that they want it. A month after that (if we're very lucky) or, in some cases, a year after that, the book will be published.

Each day, for me, I try to get myself onto a shelf before I quit. I break my book down into chapters, and I try to write one every day. I might aim for five writing days a week. I might only achieve four because of other commitments. Maybe I'll make that lost day up over the weekend. Maybe I won't. No biggie. If I'm writing five thousand words every week, then I've got 20,000 after a month. I'm producing, and my book is on track.

But, if I know I have a proper break coming up, a week or a fortnight or however long it is, I always try to get myself onto a shelf before I take that break.

The great screenwriter William Goldman said, 'Don't fire until you're ready, and then go like the clappers until you're done'. But life exists, and you're in it! Sometimes, you simply have to stop what you're doing and put your work down and go and do something more important, e.g., tending to your loved ones.

One of my writing heroes is Georges Simenon, the creator of the French detective, Maigret. Simenon was one of the most prolific and best-selling authors of all time (simply hundreds of novels, pulp novels, novellas, and short stories). Of all time! I mean, you can count on the fingers of one hand the authors who were more successful in the writing craft than him. And he may even be at the actual head of the field.

He wrote fast. Very fast. With very little research, other than an idea of a place and a few characters' names. Then he'd begin.

He could type about 100 words a minute. I can do about 30 or 40 when I'm in the zone. He would turn out a novel every month. Sometimes he'd write one in a week. No need for this guy to get on a shelf. He'd be mountain-top before he knew it.

For us mere mortals though, if we're talking about substantial creations, like novels and screenplays (and despite Noel Coward's assertion that you can write a play in a weekend), I'd say there are bound to be times when we have to take that interlude in our writing.

All I can say is, plan ahead, think about where you are going, and if you can see a break on the horizon, try not to leave yourself dangling at the end of a rope when you get there.

Get yourself on a ledge or shelf, and then you can relax and recuperate (or party like there's no tomorrow!). Ultimately, whatever you're doing, wherever you're going (and in our case, it's to be a writer), you still want and need the love and support of your friends, family, and loved ones. Don't miss that big event, don't neglect those closest to you, but position yourself to go and enjoy that event without upsetting the momentum of your project.

If you're taking a break, get yourself up on a ledge first. That way, you may eventually end up on the shelf that we all want to be on – the one in the bookstore.

So, now that we've learned when to stop writing your book, let's go and learn how to actually write one!

HOW TO WRITE A BOOK

So you've got an idea for a book. It could be a fictional novel or your memoir, or a biography of a famous person. We'll discuss each of the different types of book in their own separate chapters. For now, I'm just going to write about the act of tackling a book-length project.

Maybe you've already written a book or two, or perhaps you're about to embark on your first one. In my case, when I came to write my first book, I remember taking a deep breath as I contemplated the enormous task I had set myself. It seemed to me that I was about to begin a marathon, or attempt to climb a mountain. I knew that it would take me many months.

The thing that daunted me most, or made me most afraid, wasn't the worry about the quality of what I was going to produce. I understood, as a fairly novice writer, that I probably wouldn't have the critical faculties to judge the work as either good or bad while I was writing it. Therefore, I put that to the back of my mind.

What bothered me most was that I might set out on this journey and then lose my way, or run out of steam halfway through. That's what frightened me the most. I might spend three months writing this lengthy tome and then end up with a half-completed work. I would have failed in my goal of writing a book.

So, I decided to plot the book, chapter by chapter. I came up with about 80 chapter headings. Then, I reasoned, if I just wrote about a thousand words for each chapter, at the end of it, I'd have written a book.

I more or less knew what I was going to write about. There was a natural chronology to the story. So, I plotted each step of the journey. Then I wrote each chapter title down in a notebook until I had my 80 headings.

And then I began to write.

It didn't matter if one chapter was slightly shorter or longer than the next. I could stop at 800 words in one, and write 1500 words in the next. It didn't matter.

These chapter headings were my stepping stones. They were the path that I was going to follow.

In hindsight, I might comment that I was rather rigid in my approach. It doesn't matter. The ultimate failure of the material was due to the poor quality of the writing. It was drudgery. I was trying too hard to be a writer. I over-emphasised everything. There was no fizz. No whizz. Everything was laboured to make sure that I took the reader along with me. Except, they were all so bored that they'd probably all given up ages ago, and gone to the pub instead.

It doesn't matter, though. By following my rigid path, after about six months of writing on an almost daily basis, I had completed my novel. I had written a book.

I got a huge sense of fulfilment out of meeting that goal. I wanted to be a writer, and now I had written a book. I now knew that I could do it!

Nowadays, I think nothing of churning out a couple of books a year. I still get a huge sense of enjoyment and achievement out of it, but I am no longer daunted by the task. Having done it many times before, I know that I can do this.

But, that first book was like a stripe on my shoulder, a membership card to a club that I wanted to be a part of. It gave me a huge sense of satisfaction. I'd overcome a huge obstacle. I was no longer a wannabe writer. I had written a book.

An awful book, I'll admit, but it was still a book. The only way was up.

The next one took half the time. I was freed up, more liberated in my writing. I was still learning, but I had some muscle behind me. I could stand on my own two feet, rather than being that day-old lamb that I had been first time out.

Harper Lee's first book was *To Kill a Mockingbird*. One of the best and most-loved novels of all time. Did she ever write anything before that book? I guess she did. Was it her first attempt at a novel? I don't know. If it was, I have no idea how she did it.

Some people's first novels are great. Sometimes, it's the best book they will ever write.

If you're reading this book, you are obviously looking for a little guidance about how to go about achieving your goal. I personally think that you've got a lot more to gain by writing a plodding book that *is* a book rather than aiming for the stars and running out of steam halfway through. Your great masterpiece can come later. *Get that first book under your belt*.

You'll grow in confidence. You'll learn from the experience. And, if you have to plot it to death before you set off on the journey, then so be it. You can get cute and smart later on. For now, just get your first book written.

Stephen King says he aims to write 2000 words a day. And he writes every day. In three months, he's got a brand new 180,000-word novel. He advises novice writers not to set the bar so high, lest they get discouraged. He advises 1000 words a day, and will forgive you if you take a day off every week in which you don't write. (I'll give you two days off a week. 5,000 words a week is not a bad start). At that rate, you'll have a 60,000-word novel, perfect for an eBook, after just three months.

And the point is, *you're writing*. You're meeting your challenge head-on. Even a task as big as writing a novel can be achieved when you break it down into small enough pieces. The longest journey begins with a single step and continues one step at a time, thereafter.

That's the path you must follow. Just try and make it an interesting ride. If not first time out, you'll improve next time round. Until you get good. That's all we can do.

So finish what you've started. That's how you write a book.

HOW TO WRITE FICTION

Fiction isn't real. It's stuff you've written down that you made-up. You still need an idea to get you started, but what happens after that comes from your own imagination.

It has been said that fiction may actually be the truest form of writing because – by unleashing your subconscious, with which to tell the story – you are tapping into deeper, underlying truths, either within yourself or in society as a whole; truths that we may ordinarily wish to remain hidden or unspoken.

The beauty of fiction, for me, is that you aren't constricted by the facts of real events. You can elaborate, extenuate, accentuate, and exaggerate. You can make your characters larger than life. You can put thoughts into their heads and describe them to your reader with the all-seeing eye of an omniscient narrator. You are, basically, free to go wherever and to do whatever you want.

The only problem is, so is everybody else, so it is a very crowded marketplace. But, as we're here to learn our craft and to not necessarily count our pennies just yet, let's not worry about the competition. For now.

The aforementioned Georges Simenon was one of the most successful writers of the 20th or indeed any century. Ninety-five percent of his output was fiction. All told, he wrote some 500 books. Reviewers of the day commented that they were surprised that someone who could turn out novels at such a prolific rate could keep the standard so high. Each and every one of them was a huge bestseller.

One thing that contributed to his productivity was the lack of research involved. He would, literally on the back of an envelope, scrawl down the name of a couple of characters and the name of a town where the story would be set. And then he would be off to the typewriter.

After spending 18 months researching my book on Israel and Palestine, I fancied a bit of liberated writing myself. I thought I'd try my hand at a crime novel or a murder mystery, or something of that sort. I wanted to set my story in an exotic location, and my beautiful seaside town in the South of France fit the bill perfectly.

I needed a villain and a crime to drive my drama, and a couple of high-profile cases in Britain had recently caught my eye. So, with just a little imagination, and very little in the way of research, I began to write my work of fiction.

I hit an early stumbling block when I realised that this was effectively going to be the detective's story, and I didn't have one!

Still, as soon as the missing-girl enquiry (which was my story idea) landed at the local gendarmerie, low-and-behold a detective answered the phone, and we were then up and running.

Cause and effect appeared to be the order of the day. Something bad happened which then led to the next event on the journey, which ultimately led to our gendarme solving the crime and catching the perpetrator. Not much to it, really.

Except there is. Because what about the characters? How interesting are they? How alive do they feel to the reader? How likeable is your hero (or how flawed)? How evil is your villain (or is he a loveable rogue)? How realistic is their language? How funny and surprising are they, and does your reader want to spend time in their company?

And what about your prose? Does it leap off the page? Does it carry the reader along on the crest of a wave? Do people want to re-read paragraphs for the sheer enjoyment of what you've written, the way that your words sing like a dawn-chorus or a choir of angels?

What about your descriptions? Do they create that extra-sensory perception for a reader, so that they can almost smell the fragrance in the air or the mist or the acrid smoke? Can they almost touch the furniture, imagining themselves there?

Stephen King asks you to create three things in order to deliver a great (or even good) work of fiction: characters, dialogue, and description. They all float on the sea of prose.

I always thought that prose meant flowery language. It doesn't. It is simply the glue that holds your story together and is the essential ingredient of your book.

How do you write fiction? I would say with the freedom to write whatever you want to write, with the only limit being that of your own imagination.

We'll discuss how to get noticed and how to market yourself in due course, because fiction is probably the single biggest field in all of literature, and we can't all fit on the winner's podium.

But fiction is a great place to learn and practice your craft. You can write for sheer enjoyment and not wonder where you're headed (because only you will know where that is) and no-one can ever stop you and say 'It didn't happen like that' because it's all make-believe. It's all yours. That's fiction.

And how do you write it? Hopefully, easily and happily.

It isn't easy (damn near impossible!) to write a work of fiction like *To Kill a Mockingbird*, but it should be achievable for us to write a novel-length piece of work. Break it down into bite-sized chunks.

As I write that, I'm actually staring at the cover to E.M. Forster's *Aspects of the Novel*, where there is a picture of the author sitting hunched, head in his hands, over the tortured pages of his latest tome! But we won't let that put us off.

Consider this. In John Mullan's book *How Novels Work*, he states that 'a novel seems the easiest kind of a book for a literate person with a computer to write'. He describes a novel as 'the most accessible and democratic of literary forms'.

So, what's stopping you?

Well, there's character, story, dialogue, description, the sub-plot, beginnings, the ending, the set-ups, the set-backs, the pacing, not to mention the use of metaphor, allegory, and surrealism. You must wrestle with each word, sentence, paragraph, and chapter.

At the end of it all, though, you will have completed a novel. And I know you want to do that. You're reading this book for no other reason.

E.M. Forster talks about the story, the people, the plot, and the pattern and rhythm.

Anthony Trollope said that your book must be a pleasure to read, that your narrator must be pleasant enough for your reader to want to sit down and listen to.

Have you ever re-read a novel? Why did you do that? I'm guessing because you loved it so. What was it about that book that you loved?

One of my favourite novels is *A Stone For Danny Fisher* by Harold Robbins.

It is a tale about a young man who grows up in America's Depression and lives his life in the manner that most of us would aspire to. Find love, live comfortably, overcome our obstacles, achieve our goals. It is a cradle-to-grave story, and we root for Danny, our protagonist, as life continually tries to scupper his dreams.

It is told in the first person. You really only have two choices when it comes to telling your story.

First-person, from somebody's (usually the main character's) point of view.

Third-person, as the all-seeing narrator, observing from above and describing what you see.

Why not try the opening chapter or page of your own book in both styles to see which one feels right and works best for you. I (and others) would say that third-person narration generally has prevalence, and that's probably for a good reason. It just works, that's all, and it gives you a little space to sit back and describe the action.

Ultimately, you need to deliver a story that your audience can lose themselves in. That's what *you* love about the stories that you read.

Your audience wants to find the same things in the books that you write. It's not rocket science, is it? It's just storytelling.

You need to be authoritative. Think of the word. Author-itative.

Basically, it means being in charge. You are in charge of the situation. You've invited your audience, by means of that attractive book cover and the accompanying blurb, not to mention the well-thought-out and (possibly) well-financed publicity campaign, to sit down at your knee and to listen to your story.

What are you going to do when they get there? What do you have to offer?

You are the author. You are the boss.

Having grabbed the audience that you want, are you really going to trail off after a few minutes in the absence of meaning and direction? No. You're going to try your best to keep them enthralled while you regale them with the tale that you've given up a lot of your free time to create.

And don't think that you'll just sit down at the computer to write, and it will then just pour out of you without any effort on your part. We'll get to how difficult *that* is in a short while. For now, it's enough to understand that you might have to go over your work many times in order to bring it up to the required standard.

One adage in our craft is that *writing is re-writing*.

You're going to need a cover for that book of yours at some point, but that's just the icing on the cake. The cake needs an opening line.

'It was the best of times. It was the worst of times'. That's a good one.

Immediately it gets the audience thinking, and involved. What does the author mean by that? The reader wants to know more. It's a hook.

Are you going to stop there? How about keeping that interest going for the remainder of the opening paragraph, page, chapter, or even book. It's a challenge. Are you up to it?

What about the ending? Happy or sad? What is the goal of each individual scene or chapter? Does it keep moving? Does it constantly deliver?

Remember, your readers will wander off if you allow them to. They have lives and loved ones waiting in the wings. It's your duty to keep them listening, and they will, as long as you don't let reality intervene between your storytelling voice and their own focused minds.

Your voice as a writer is one of your most powerful tools. What does it mean? Essentially, I think it's the voice that the reader hears in their head as they listen to your story. Is it lively, engaging, forceful, sympathetic, interesting?

It better be *something* as, without a voice, there's not much for an audience to listen to.

Your story may well have a theme, something sunken beneath the surface that keeps people thinking about it once they've turned the last page. Your book can, and should, touch your reader on so many levels. It should interest and move them, make them think, make them laugh or cry. Maybe even both.

And that character you've chosen as your protagonist, they have obviously inspired you – the author – in some way. Never lose sight of what they mean to you.

They may be the writer in disguise. We can't help it. We put ourselves into the stories that we create. We write what we know to some extent. Try to enjoy it and show off your best. When we get to know a bit more about the writer (e.g., when you become rich and famous), we'll probably be able to identify the parts that correlate to your real-life anyway. Go with it. Let the story be the boss, and if you end up in there too, then so be it.

There are no limits to what you can write in fiction. You can have 500 tanks coming over the hill, or 500 camels, or 500 spaceships for that matter. It costs nothing to write, so let loose your imagination. Tell your story.

It's fiction. It's all false. You can deny everything after the fact.

Irvine Welsh has written a number of best-selling books. His first was *Trainspotting*.

It was a fictionalised account of a group of heroin addicts in Edinburgh. Irvine is from Edinburgh. He's more than dabbled in drugs. The tale he created featured characters similar to friends and people that he knew. The central character, Rent Boy, was probably the character who most resembled himself, and served as the writer in disguise. Still, it featured events that never happened, and a narrative that – in all probability – didn't exist, but that worked exceedingly well as a story.

I went to a writer's conference in my home town, and Irvine Welsh was there talking about the unexpected success of his gritty novel. He said that he'd bumped into an old friend one day, someone who had read the book.

So true was the story, the setting, and the characters, that his old friend admonished him with the words 'You made half of that up!'

You can't make *that* up.

Go where the fiction takes you. And you'll be in there somewhere, and I don't just mean your name on the cover. It's your book. Your story. We're waiting.

And do you know what it is that we're waiting for?

What follows are probably the three most important words that you will read in this book. What your audience wants to know, what keeps an audience listening and reading, is that they need to know '*What happens next?*'

That's the key. That's more important than style or substance, dialogue or description. If you can keep your reader hanging on in anticipation of that one vital ingredient, you'll always have an audience.

And you'll have a story. You'll have a novel. You'll be a writer.

EXERCISES

We've discussed a lot of theory so far, and there's still plenty of that to come, but as writing is an active and not a passive pastime, here's a few exercises to help you put theory into practice.

In order to know what it is that you're writing about, and before you set out on that lengthy journey, try and answer the following questions or perform these activities.

Your responses will give you a good overview of your book or script.

1. Describe the story in 20 words or less (e.g., a murder mystery set in London involving…).
2. Now elaborate and describe the story in 100 words or less (e.g., set in London, the book follows the story of the main character who, etc…).
3. Describe the three primary characteristics of the main character.
4. Describe three aspects of the main antagonist / villain of the piece.
5. Name three obstacles that the main character must overcome in order to achieve their goal.
6. Think of three alternative titles for your new book, script, or play.

7. Write a paragraph of prose that calls upon as many of the senses that you can describe. You'll want to create a sensory perception for your reader, so can you employ sounds, smells, and tastes in your description of a scene.
8. Describe a room or a place in your story, giving enough information to allow the reader to visualise the setting in their mind.
9. Imagine if you were a character in a story. How would you describe yourself and the room where you are sitting right now, as if you were describing it in a book?
10. Write a quarrel scene between two of your characters (or two new characters). Look for nuanced, clever and original ways for them to work through their dispute without just having a shouting contest.
11. Think of a 'what if' idea, no matter how ludicrous it may seem.
12. Expand your 'what if' idea into a one-page outline, including characters and setting.
13. Write a short (one or two pages) re-telling of a story you know well (like a film or a fairy tale) from a different character's perspective. (e.g., write *Snow White* from the Wicked Witch's point of view)
14. Write a short outline of your novel, play, or screenplay, from another character's (e.g., not your main character's) perspective.
15. Write a short biography for each of the main protagonists in your story, e.g., how old they are, what they look like, where they went to school, what do they like to eat, hobbies and interests.

The more you understand your characters, the better you can describe their surroundings, the more lively and interesting your dialogue, and the better developed your plot and more rewarding your work will be. Use the exercises above to get the most out of, and into, your story.

HOW TO WRITE NON-FICTION

I like non-fiction. For me, stories have more weight if I know that they are true. But that's just my own personal taste.

There's nothing to say that a non-fiction book can't be as exciting or as dramatic as a novel. There's no rule against you making it as interesting as anything else ever written. In fact, writers such as Truman Capote with *In Cold Blood* and Norman Mailer with *The Executioner's Song* wrote books so riveting that literary critics had to coin a new phrase for their work: the *non-fiction novel*.

Think of a book such as Mark Bowden's *Black Hawk Down*. That's non-fiction. Or the same author's *Killing Pablo* about the rise and fall of drugs mogul Pablo Escobar. Absolutely riveting. Absolutely factual. Absolutely non-fiction.

So, how do you write non-fiction?

Well, what you're writing is purporting to be the truth, so you better have all of your facts to hand. In order to do that, unless you were at every event that you are describing (and you are blessed with perfect recall), then you are going to have to do a lot of research.

Be prepared to spend a lot of time in the library, to read a lot of books on the subject or about the characters involved. Maybe read up on the era about which you are writing in order to give context to your story.

As I've mentioned previously in this book, I once wrote a history of Israel and Palestine, a subject that I knew absolutely nothing about. How dare he, I hear you say. Well, I wrote the book for me, to educate myself about a subject that I was intrigued by yet didn't really understand.

In preparation, I read the Bible, books on archaeology, and others on Ancient Egypt. I read Sigmund Freud *Moses and Monotheism* so that you didn't have to! I searched the internet. I ended up with ten shoe-boxes full of research material, and I read it all, and then I organised it chronologically. And after 18 months of research, I began to write down my findings.

A year after that, I'd put those findings into a book. Six months after that, I self-published 1000 copies at a cost of £2000. I sold them to friends and family and to independent bookshops. Five years later, I published an eBook version. Seven years after that, a professional publisher picked it up.

That book now outranks Noam Chomsky's own work on the same subject, and he's one of the world's most eminent academics.

Am I an authority? No, just an enthusiastic amateur.

I would say that you could write about any subject that interests you (otherwise what's the point, right?) as long as you do the necessary research.

Know what you're talking about, by putting in the requisite hours to learn all about it, and then tell the audience the facts using all of your storytelling skills.

Non-fiction doesn't have to mean a textbook. It can be a true-life account of any subject that can be as riveting as any other work.

Jon Ronson writes quirky books on subjects that interest him. One of them, *The Men Who Stare at Goats* was turned into a movie with George Clooney. If Hollywood doesn't turn its up nose at non-fiction, then neither should we!

One of my all-time favourite books is Dee Brown's *Bury my heart at Wounded Knee*, which describes itself as an Indian history of the American West. The book moved me emotionally, almost to tears.

Brown spent the early part of his life working in the lumber camps and oil fields of the American South West. He later worked as a printer, journalist, and librarian. He wrote several books about the history of the Old West, and was haunted by the tragic story of the American Indians. His *Wounded Knee* book was the result of many years of research in which he sought to set the record straight about the fate of the indigenous people of the United States.

In 2007, the Pulitzer Prize for non-fiction went to Lawrence Wright's *The Looming Tower*, which told in fine detail the story of Al Qaeda's road to 9/11 and the destruction of the Twin Towers at the World Trade Centre in New York. Critics described the book as beautifully written and wonderfully compelling. They said that it worked as a thriller as well as a tragedy, and was both devastating and terrifying. Wright was praised for having created a work that was forensic in its detail, and one that was told with the stripped-down prose of a thriller writer. It was, according to one review, a masterful combination of reporting and writing.

That, I think, sums up your task in a nutshell. Reporting and writing. In order to report, you must carry out the requisite research. When I wrote my history of Israel and Palestine, I would read a bit (or a lot), and then write a bit. You have to make yourself an authority on the subject you are going to cover.

Readers expect to learn something. They want to know what special insights you – the writer – are about to divulge. Your job is to explore the unknown territory and to report back. You're a scout, an advance reconnaissance party (of, usually, one).

Two books that recently topped the non-fiction charts are *The Secret Barrister* and *This is going to hurt*, told by a barrister and a junior doctor, respectively.

Both books were written by people who had inside knowledge of their subject, and each writer delivered an acerbic, humorous, intelligent, and passionate portrayal of the fields in which they were employed.

They highlighted the shortcomings and contradictions that they encountered on a daily basis, and gave the reader a peek behind the curtain, as it were, to show a picture of life as it really is for people working in those professions.

Their audience was not limited to their peers in their chosen industries. They touched a nerve with the general public and enjoyed sales that earned both of them 'best-seller' status.

A writer may choose to spend some or all of their career writing nothing but non-fiction. They can still employ all of their imagination, creativity, and power of word-play to deliver gripping works that move and resonate with their readers.

The Looming Tower was recently turned into a ten-part television series. The book became source material for the dramatists who followed in the original author's footsteps.

Should you come to work in the field of non-fiction, your options are as unlimited as those that exist for fiction, and your responsibility as a storyteller will be similarly undiminished. Just tell your story – true or false – to the best of your ability.

HOW TO WRITE A MEMOIR

So, what's the difference between a memoir and an autobiography? Well, if you write an autobiography, it is generally going to cover the whole of your life up to the time in which you are writing. Some people might even divide theirs into parts one, two, and three, but those are usually reserved for either the very famous or the very vain.

For most of us, one autobiography will suffice. In it, you will cover your birth, your parents, your childhood, adolescence, early adulthood, middle age, and up to (and including) your older years. That's all of your life right there in a book, and that's your autobiography.

A memoir, on the other hand, is simply the story of a particular time in your life. The word comes from the French 'memoire', meaning either your memory itself or a specific memory. That's all a memoir is: a particular memory, of a time or place or person that you spent time with.

Let's put it like this. You can probably only write one autobiography, but you could write *lots* of memoirs.

I've written two of the latter. Both were very early in my writing career. Neither have been published, and even in this golden age of self-publication, I doubt that either of them deserve to be put on display. Still, I got something out of my system by writing them, and they all added up towards my 10,000 hours of writing practice.

My first was a childhood memoir. We actually moved to a new house in a new town when I was ten-years-old. I wanted to recapture that golden time in my first childhood home, when everything was either school-time or play-time, and the worries and cares of life were still a million miles away. I took ten years of memories and condensed them into a single calendar year. After all, I didn't want to run out of story matter.

Some events, such as Bonfire Night or the build-up to Christmas, slotted into their obvious months, as did Easter, the summer holidays, and the like. Whatever memories I had leftover, I could sprinkle evenly throughout the remainder of the year, giving an even-handed weight to the book. I gave it the title of *Mousy*, which was my childhood nickname. I also turned it into a movie screenplay, which got a little attention. Then I put it in the bottom drawer where it probably sits to this day.

My next memoir was about a particular summer when my life was seemingly going nowhere, but where I had also latched onto the idea of heading off to university.

It was about casting off the old me and embracing the new, as my life was about to change direction. The transition had proved, in reality, quite difficult. My old ways and my new were like two different worlds.

For a period of one summer (it was probably more like 18 months but, in the book, I packed it into three), I tried to walk the tightrope between these two worlds as I sought to turn my life around.

Actually, as I'm writing this, I've just remembered that the two books came the other way round, the summer memoir first and the childhood memoir later. It doesn't really matter. They both ended up in that same bottom drawer. Which one is on top, or which one came first, is of little interest to you, me, or anyone else. I have no wish to re-visit them. That's where they'll stay.

Why would you want to write a memoir? Well, I guess for most people, they want to write it down before they forget it. They want to capture, and preserve, that special memory. It might be the story of first love, or a magical summer, or of a unique achievement.

The writer might also consider that – if it was important to them – then it might also be important to other people. They might think of it as preserving something like a learned skill, such as blacksmithing, that is in danger of dying out. They might want to write it down to record it for future generations.

How do you write a memoir? Well, before you sit down to write, you have to afford yourself the time and space to think about *what it is* that you want to say.

You have to summon up all of those memories from the deep recesses of your subconscious mind. You need to wring that sponge, dig into each forgotten corner, and remember everything that you can about the event, person, place, or time about which you want to write.

Your reasons for writing a memoir can be numerous. You might want to gain or bring closure or healing about an event, person, time, or place. The tone of your book might be humorous, or alternatively dark and serious.

Who are you writing the book for? Is it for yourself, or is it for publication? Do you hope (as lots of us do) that it sells a million copies and is therefore aimed at the mass-market? If so, what is so special about you or about the time or place or event about which you're writing? Do you have a snazzy title for it? That will certainly help attract the attention of a publisher or make you stand out from the crowd if you're self-publishing.

Does your book have a theme, by which I mean it strikes some chord and touches an audience (or at least is meant to) on a more subconscious level?

And what about naming other people (i.e., real people), in your work? What are the ethics involved in that? Well, as far as I'm aware, unless you're going to libel someone or damage their reputation and their ability to earn a living in some way, then there is no bar to you naming names. But how will they feel about it? You'll have to be the judge of that or live with the consequences. In the UK, you need to be very conscious of libel. It is up to you if it comes to court, to prove that something is *not* libellous. In turn, even if you use a made-up name, if that person – in real-life – can be identified by readers, you might have a problem.

I once asked Howard Marks, author of the bestselling book *Mr Nice*, about all of the people he had named in his work. After all, he was confessing to doing enormous drug deals with these people. His response was that no one he had mentioned in the book had ever complained. The only people who *had* complained were the ones that he had failed to mention!

I guess you can never really tell how people will react. Maybe that old adage should apply, if you can't say something nice about someone, then say nothing.

At the end of the day, it's your version of events. Does that make it true? It's certainly how you remember it, so you have the moral right to say it. And there's nothing stopping someone else giving their own version of events to counter yours.

Just remember that you might be writing about the living. If so, respect their feelings and understand that they have a right of reply. Factor that into your writing.

And even more so if you're writing about close friends or family. Do you really want to upset *those* guys? Not worth it, not even for a million book sales.

What makes a good memoir? Chris Stewart wrote a book called *Driving Over Lemons* about his time spent buying and renovating an old property in Spain. The writer had been the original drummer with the band Genesis. He had left and been replaced by Phil Collins. That fact was pounded to death by his publisher and publicist, and it did no harm to his sales.

Peter Mayles had similar success with *A Year in Provence*.

Tony Hawks, a well-known stand-up comedian, wrote a memoir about his travels around Ireland with a fridge. Obviously, the book was intended to be humorous and not too heavy. It sold half a million copies. If he made a quid on each book, then he didn't do half bad, did he? They even turned it into a movie.

And then there are the misery-memoirs, a whole genre that yielded such Blockbusters as Frank McCourt's *Angela's Ashes,* or *A Child called It* by

Dave Pelzer. It seems that it is possible to turn even the worst of times into material for your bestselling book.

Remember, *your* memoir is *your* personal memory of a person, time, or place. If you want the rest of us to read it, you should give us a good reason to do so. You can try humour, try pain, try whatever you want, but try to tell a good story.

Without that, well, there's always that bottom drawer.

HOW TO WRITE A BIOGRAPHY

How do you tell someone else's story? Are you planning to write an official biography (i.e., one with the subject's permission) or an unauthorised one (i.e., publish and be damned)?

Author Albert Goldman once wrote a book about John Lennon, the former Beatle and famous musician. Goldman had actually included the quote 'Utter crap' by Paul McCartney on the back of the book, as if that leant it more credence or made it somehow more notorious. I have to say – having read the book – that I'm in agreement with Sir Paul's verdict.

My thoughts upon finishing the book were, 'Why would you?' Why would you spend maybe a year researching and then another year writing a book about a subject that you obviously had no affection for? Unless Lennon had done something so awful to the author that he wanted to destroy his public persona, why would he have put himself to that much trouble to perform such a hatchet-job on a much-loved figure?

Obviously, money is a factor. Perhaps it was the only one.

I personally hope that no one reading these pages would ever give up two years of their life on such a terrible crusade. If you're going to write a book about someone other than yourself, please try and keep your motives pure. Even if you're writing for money, choose a subject matter or person that you either admire or can empathise with. Otherwise, you'll be miserable company for the duration of the enterprise.

To state the bleeding obvious. An autobiography is you telling your own story. A biography is when an author writes about someone else. The subject of a biography will, in all likelihood, be famous, or at least deserving of recognition.

You may choose to open the book with some tragic or notable event that occurs towards the end of that person's life, as a suitably dramatic opening and a precursor of things to come. Then, you go back to the beginning and tell that person's life in pretty-much chronological order.

You'll explain their origins and ancestors, and the times and circumstances into which they were born. You'll detail their early years. You'll show the first shoots of talent emerging from their surroundings. You'll chronicle their struggle to break through to the big time.

Then, you'll detail their inexorable rise to the top. Their finding of love. The marriage, children, affairs, escapades.

There'll be time for diversions into the lives of their showbiz pals, and an exploration of opportunities won and lost.

You'll capture their darker moments, their run-ins with the Press and with their peers. All in all, you'll detail the life of a (probably) well-known figure.

I once read an obituary of a famous newspaper editor. (Obituaries, by the way, deliver great potted histories. Apart from the sadness inherent in their content, they are also super-condensed biographies).

In this particular obituary, it said that the subject had once been asked to write his autobiography for publication by a well-known publishing house.

He accepted the offer and then spent a couple of years working on the manuscript, describing all of the famous people he had met, and the momentous events he had been a part of, or that he had described within the journalism of his esteemed newspaper.

His publisher read through the copy and then asked for a meeting.

At their rendezvous, the publisher said to the writer, 'This is all very interesting, but tell me, were you never married?'

In his haste to describe how fascinating his working life had been, the author had neglected to mention his wife, who was also the mother of his children, or those children themselves, who each had their own hopes and dreams and whose lives must have impacted heavily upon his own. Rather one-sighted that one. Try to paint a well-rounded picture of your subject. After all, no man, or woman, is an island.

One could take a more erudite approach. Norman Mailer wrote a biography of Marilyn Monroe. In it, he is like an art critic, studying his prey as if it were a bronze statue or a Cubist painting, his mind pouring out thoughts as he weighs up meaning.

It is a sparring contest, in which Mailer's lyricism is used to describe the 20th-century icon he has challenged himself to uncover. The ebb and flow of her life are matched by the web and weave of his own way with words.

A more recent biography had Prince Charles as its subject. One look at the index showed the direction that the book would take. Under 'Prince Charles' it had sub-headings for his eccentricities, meanness, nastiness, and betrayals. The theme of the book, obviously, was to denigrate its subject. Again, why bother? You can be commissioned to write a biography, but I believe that both you and your publisher should look to marry you up to a subject that you have the heart and the desire to write about. No book is ever an easy feat (though some are a lot easier than others). At least do yourself the service of trying to make it a labour of love.

I recently wrote a biography of Tommy Cooper. I had approached several publishers about my self-published works which were doing well in the marketplace. One of them read my literary CV and suggested that I write a Cooper biography. They then asked for a chapter breakdown, and asked what could I bring to a new biography on the subject?

Well, I had written a hit play on the subject, so that gave me a bit of credence. I was also willing to work without pay, which gave me another in! I have always written without payment or commission. It's what we writer's do, up to the point when we no longer have to.

What else could I offer my publisher and the eventual reader that would make me suitable for the role of Cooper's biographer? Well, the archive of all of the comedian's material had just been donated to the Victoria and Albert Museum.

It would not be available to the general public for a year or so after the book was due for publication.

I'd previously worked on the restoration of the Albert Memorial, working with specialist conservationists and documenters from the V&A. I wrote to them (emailed them, in fact) and explained about my book deal and my pending deadline. I told them about my restoration work on the Albert Memorial and my close ties with the V&A, and about my training in the ethics of conservation, which meant I would not ride roughshod over the archive that they were still in the process of cataloguing.

They agreed to my request, and I was granted privileged and advance access to the material. Now, when anyone asked what unique selling points my book would have, my publisher and I could state that it was written by the creator of the hit, touring Tommy Cooper play, and that I was also the first member of the British public to be given access to the Tommy Cooper archive at the V & A.

What's *your* unique selling point to the subject of your biography? Or, like Mailer's biography of Monroe, is your exemplary writing style the thing that sets your book apart?

Ultimately, you're writing non-fiction about a real person. Tell us why they hold you in such thrall.

Try to keep a modicum of art in what you do. After all, your whole apprenticeship has been about learning your craft. This artistic sensibility sustained you through months and years of rejection. You kept going because you believed in your writing and because you believe that writing is what you were put on this earth to do.

You can still show us some of *your* story, even as you are telling us *their* story. And that, I think, is how you write a biography.

HOW TO WRITE A MANUAL

I'm sure most of you reading this book share my dream of being a literary writer. It may be, though, that for some of you, writing is simply a means to an end. You have some knowledge that you wish to pass on. You are an expert in your field or have some particular know-how that you want to share with an audience.

How best to communicate that knowledge? Well, a good way to do it is through a manual or a 'how-to' book.

You could say that you are holding one such book in your hands right now.

So, if your aim is to produce one of your own, how do you go about it?

Well, I've written three manuals, including the one that you're currently reading. This one, obviously, is about writing. Another was *The Quantity Surveyor's Bible* detailing the ins and outs of the day job that I have done for over 20 years. The other was called *Serious about learning French*.

Am I fluent in French? Have I mastered French as a second language? The answer is no, and I confessed as much in the introduction to the book. What I am an expert at, however, is *attempting* to learn French. (Please, no sniggering at the back).

I have studied French at school, college, university (for a year), at night-school, in informal groups, and at language school in Nice. I have taught a beginner's French group, and while I have only a minor understanding of the language myself, I believe I can guide others on their journey by having attempted to learn French in so many different teaching environments.

So, while not claiming to be an expert in the subject, I am pretty well-versed in how to go about learning it. A real language expert would (and they have!) spot several faux-pas within the text of my book, but it is, I believe, a less intimidating work than many others on the subject. After all, if you're going to learn a language, you're going to make mistakes. Sometimes you feel more comfortable learning alongside someone who's only halfway there themselves. Not everyone wants to practice their tennis with Boris Becker or their golf with Tiger Woods!

Basically, I believed that I had spotted some flaws in the way that the language was taught. I had a passion for the subject, and I wanted to encourage people and also point out the pitfalls that I'd identified in the various teaching methods I'd encountered. I could consolidate all of my learning in a single place, and also write another book in the process!

But I couldn't just write a 'how-to' book about anything. *Beekeeping* by Ian Carroll, anyone? Not going to happen. Not unless I take up the subject and research it properly and have a reason to write it.

A manual should be written by an expert in the field, or at least by someone with a passion for, and an understanding of, the subject.

Looking along my own bookshelf, there is one about writing penned by three of the professors at the university where I did my Master's degree. It was recommended reading for the course. The letters after their names probably filled up the first half-dozen pages.

There is a line in the introduction that states:

'This is a book for people determined to write'.

We can sometimes lose sight (us writers) of just how determined we are. It is a calling. It's *our* calling. It's nice to be reminded of that and, I suppose, praised for it every now and then.

Then, in my library, there is a screenwriting book written by a Doctor with 20 years' experience in the field, working with major and independent film studios and television networks. The author has taught writing and media/communications at the American Film Institute and has a Ph.D. in Media Ecology (whatever that means!). You just know that you are in good hands.

There is also a law book on my shelves written by a barrister of Grays Inn, London, who is also the Pro-Vice-Chancellor of the University of Oxford and a Professor of English Private Law. He is LLB, BCL, and MA qualified. Again, a safe pair of hands.

Finally, there is a South Indian cookbook. What it is doing there in my library is a mystery. It came as a freebie from a well-known supermarket and probably, because I'm a writer, I could not bring myself to consign the book to a bin.

I don't think I will ever attempt a single recipe from within its pages, for the simple reason that I am – at best – a very moderate cook. The author was born in India, despite being raised in England, and lived for ten years in one of the regions that she writes about. She has written books on Malaysian and Indian cooking, and teaches Indian cooking at an adult-education centre. She clearly has a passion for her subject, and has the knowledge to render her a suitable guide.

If you wish to write a manual or a 'how-to' book, what is your own area of expertise? Why is your book going to be different from those already out there? How is yours going to stand out from the crowd?

Share your individual knowledge and expertise. It's also a great excuse to write your next book. After all, we're writers, first and foremost.

Do your research. Try and find any gaps that exist in the current market. If you're fluent in Greek, having learned it as a second language, and there only one or two books available on the subject, that sounds like there could well be room for yours.

If the most recent book published on a particular topic was several years ago, maybe it's time to introduce something fresh and modern,

What information are people looking for? Can you explore forums and other online discussions to see if people are craving advice or support on a particular topic?

My own sister is a schoolteacher. She told me recently that there is a dearth of 'issue-based' stories for kids. They want to cover topics such as bullying, and how better to do that than through a traditional children's storybook.

Find those gaps. Write your book.

Set it out with the same forethought as you would any other book. What is the most interesting way that I can structure my book? What does the reader need to know, and in what order?

If you fail to engage and motivate, how are you ever going to hold their attention as you try to impart the knowledge that you've come to deliver.

Utilise your experience. Of your subject and your writing. Your audience, and your pupils, await.

HOW TO WRITE IN 'FREE-FLOW'

Probably the greatest fear for a writer is that they sit down at the computer and then nothing comes out. No matter how hard you might rack your brains, there's just nothing there. There's nothing in the imagination or the locker that you can unleash onto the page. You have writer's block, or you are merely stumped – literally – for words.

I'm not quite sure what the cure for writer's block is. Some say a day job. If you're kept at bay from the thing you're desperate to do then, come the opportunity, you will seize it with both hands.

So, if the absence of output is the great fear of every writer, how do we attain Nirvana? How do we reach that inspired state where the words are pouring out of us at a rate of 30, 40, or 50 words a minute, when our fingers are racing to try to keep up with our brains, and when there's smoke coming out of the keyboard because we're typing that fast?

Well, routine is a good way to create momentum. If you give yourself an hour a day to write, or set yourself a target of 1000 words, then that can help.

Your subconscious will come to expect you to be at your computer at a certain time or for a certain amount of time. It will come to appreciate the exercise and the opportunity to unburden itself of all that it has gathered up since your last session. While you've been working, sleeping, and eating – and all of the things that your life entails – your inner mind will know that it has work to do, and that you will soon be calling it to action. And it will be there, waiting for you; so all you have to do is put your bum in a chair and begin.

I have my own personal tip for you, to help you get into that free-flow zone, where you feel like you are simply channelling the words, as if someone else is creating them and you are merely that creator's stenographer.

Write about what you know. That is a popular maxim for writing anyway, but I mean it in a slightly different way. When you choose to write about a subject with which you are intimately acquainted, you can find yourself liberated.

This book you're reading right now is a case in point. I'd had some success with my book on Quantity Surveying. I knew my day job *inside out*. I had 25 years' experience in the field. So, I wrote down 50 chapter headings that would encompass this particular profession, then all I had to do was write approximately 1000 words for each chapter. Hey presto! I had a book.

I thought, well that was easy enough. What else can I write about where I have enough knowledge of the subject that I can just sit down and write? I wanted to get into that free-flow zone. It meant that all of my time spent writing would be exactly that. I wouldn't have to do an inordinate amount of preparation. I could just write what I knew.

I had 30 years of writing experience to call upon. I had a passion for the subject that would hopefully transfer to the page. I'd had my ups and downs over those many years of practice and study. I had hopefully learned my craft. I'd even, finally, had some success.

All I had to do was write down 50 chapter headings that would give a well-rounded view of the subject and then put my bum on a chair and write it.

You can do the same. I've written books that have involved years of research before I could put pen to paper, and others, such as this, where I was able to quickly get the venture underway in terms of putting pen to paper.

To be honest, after this one, I've probably exhausted all of the subjects that I can just sit down and write about, but it's another book published, another one 'out there', and another one of which I hope I can be suitably proud.

The more you write, the easier it will be to get into your stride. Exhaust your own passions and experiences. See if there's a book in there for you. Keep us rapt. And keep on writing.

HOW TO BE A GHOST-WRITER

What is a ghost-writer? Well, it's not someone who writes ghost or horror stories. It is basically someone who writes something on behalf of someone else, leaves their name off the work, and allows the other person to take all of the credit.

Why would you write something and not put your name to it? Well, for the money, of course!

Basically, while you are learning your craft, you might write a few introspective pieces to maybe give yourself closure after an event, or maybe as catharsis, or even just to get some words down on paper that serve towards your 10,000 hours of training. Essentially, I'm talking about that stage in your career when you are writing for yourself: when you have no expectation to sell your work.

Then, when you've arrived at a place where you more or less know what you're doing, and are a writer of some ability, you are only ever writing for one of two reasons: for praise or prosperity. Maybe you even want both: fame *and* fortune.

Believe me, if you're getting neither from something you've written, by the time that you have learned your craft and know what you're doing, then you're being ripped off. Take it from me. I know.

Is there something unethical about being a ghost-writer? Possibly. Slightly. Yet only in certain circumstances. For the most part, it is a recognised avenue for your writing, and can provide some much-needed revenue.

A lot of people, particularly famous people, get offered lucrative book deals. But, guess what, they usually don't know how to write a book. Michael Owen, the ex-footballer, for one, claims never to have read a single book in his life! That may be an old quote. He may by now be an avid reader. Yet, at the time that he said it, I'm sure that he meant it. Such was his devotion to putting his footballing talent on the stage that it deserved, he had no time to read about anyone or anything else. He was chasing and then living the dream. What use did he have for someone else's fiction?

So, I get it. But, I know that Michael has written a book, or at least has had a book published that purports to be his 'autobiography'. But, how can he write a book when he is too busy to even read one? And, if he's never read one, how's he ever going to know how to write one?

If there's an offer of half a million pounds on the table though, I'm sure that there's a way. And the way that it's done is that the publisher will assign Michael Owen a ghost-writer (actually, in his case, it was Mark

Eglinton), and they will be tasked with picking Michael's brain over the course of several interviews and then going away and doing some research and turning all of that source material into a book that will (hopefully) be a Christmas bestseller.

Usain Bolt has an autobiography out called *Faster than Lightning*. Inside the front cover, it states that 'Usain Bolt exerts his moral right to be identified as the author of this work'. Do I believe for a minute that he wrote it? In fact, I believe it for less time than it takes him to run the 100 metres.

Look through the list of acknowledgements in the back of Bolt's book and you find a thank you to a certain Matt Allen for 'getting my story onto the page'.

Do an internet search for Matt Allen, author, and you find he has a literary agent and there, in the list of his published works, you find the book he has written for Usain Bolt. If he's not getting credit on the cover for having written the book, you know that he's certainly getting paid.

Being a ghost-writer means that you are a writer for hire. No shame in that. It saves the problem of wondering *what* to write. You've got a project, an assignment, and you're getting paid!

You can hone certain skills, e.g., in research, interview techniques, collating information, driving a narrative that isn't your own. And, you'll be working with professional people, maybe rubbing shoulders with a celebrity, and dealing with publishers and editors and marketing personnel, and also meeting deadlines.

You'll need to develop interview techniques. Where are you going to meet? Are you going to Skype? Are you going to present a set of questions to your subject and ask them to answer them? Are you going to tape your interviews if they are face to face or Skyped or conference-called? It's probably a good idea to have a record of your conversations that you can refer back to.

That leads to the consideration of equipment. Do you have an audio device that will record your interview? If not, you probably need to buy one. A good one. No point using something that isn't going to do the job that you want it to.

And what questions are you going to ask? Where did you go to school? When did you get your first break? What was the biggest set-back you encountered, and how did you overcome that obstacle?

Are you going to throw them a curve-ball to give your narrative an added dimension?

Think about what you want to find out about your subject, and how best to go about obtaining the information that you need.

You probably need to set up a series of interviews or question and answer sessions. If you have a 12-month deadline for your book, maybe you need to have one of these sessions every month for the first 6 months before you set off alone on the writing phase.

You could maybe make each monthly session coincide with a stage of that person's life, i.e., month 1 – early years. Month 2 – adolescence to adulthood. Month 3 – family and parenthood etc.

Get organised. Gather your info. Get writing.

In all, you'll be doing what you really want to do, by which I mean writing, and you'll be doing it for a living.

How do you come by this potentially lucrative work? Well, getting an agent seems like a good way. These people will be aware of what's happening in the marketplace, which celebrities have been offered book deals, and which projects are still in search of a writer. They will act as matchmakers. Your experience, credentials, and profile will be the criteria that they judge you on, should your name even come close to being considered.

Other avenues for ghost-writers include screenwriting. Lots of writers get brought in to work on other people's scripts. Again, if you're not getting a writing credit, make sure you're compensated in other ways, by which I mean sufficient remuneration. It can only ever be one or the other. Sometimes you want or get both – fame and fortune. Make sure you get at least one or, like I've said, you're being ripped off, and no one wants that.

Essay writing is another form of ghost-writing. It's an apparently growing field, but one even more mired in ethical issues. Should you help someone pass an exam or gain a qualification by submitting work you've carried out on their behalf?

I've done it (only for one person), so I can't claim any moral high-ground here. I did it for money (shame on you, I hear you say). He was a friend of a good friend, and he needed a bit of help as he wanted to focus on the practical aspect of his course (in filmmaking) and was struggling to keep up with the theoretical.

All I can say in my defence is, I wouldn't write an essay on brain-surgery that would allow someone to go and practice while not suitably qualified. No one's life is going to be on the line for what I've done. On the plus side, we may have a new film-maker in our midst. Maybe next time, he'll ask for my help on the screenplay for his first feature film.

Ghost-writing, in all of its forms, appears to be a growing field, so whatever the ethical issues, I guess there's something in it for us writers.

Just make sure you ask yourself that moral question before you accept the commission, in case you ever need that brain surgeon!

EACH FORMAT IS A DIFFERENT LANGUAGE

As writers, we are artists. As artists, we are creators. As creative people, we cherish freedom and individuality, but we'd better get used to the fact that the buying public will want to get a handle on who we are and what it is that we do.

I'd like to think that you or I could jump from writing horror to comedy, and then to crime, to biography, and still take our audience along with us. After all, no one tells Blur that they can't sing a slow song because their last one was poppy or grunge. If it's good, it's good. But people like to put you in a box and categorise you, and your work has to sit somewhere in the bookshop.

They want you to help them by sticking to one style. Maybe booksellers should perhaps list all books alphabetically by author and then let the public decide what they want? But that's just me being idealistic.

By format, I mean medium. How do you move from the world of theatre, to film, to book, and still maintain mastery of the form? Well, I would answer (my own question!) by saying that they all have their own particular sets of requirements, and each has to be mastered in turn. Think of them as different languages, but it is all still communication.

And when it comes to languages, human beings like shortcuts and, if it is possible for a two-year-old child to start to pick up a language, then you'd better believe that there are shortcuts to be had.

Similarly, in your writing, there will be many transferable skills that you can take with you when moving from one format to another. That doesn't mean that you don't have to put in the hours to learn the basics and then progress from there, but you can take a lot of that learned stuff with you as you move between different media.

When you learn to be a writer, don't limit yourself to one discipline. Just because you've written a book, don't be afraid to try writing in a different form. You might find moving between fields a little cumbersome at first. It might be a bit slow-going. You'll wonder why you're back at the beginning, learning a new discipline when you were already so far down the road writing in a different format.

However, if you feel your next story would work better as, say, a play or a radio play, look in your kit-bag of learned things. You'll find you already have many of the skills with which to tell your story in another format.

Say you've started out as a novelist, and now you want to write a play. How do you go about it?

With a novel, you're writing prose. It's one word after another. You're inside the character's mind, or floating above and describing the action. It's a story told in thoughts.

With a play, you have to write for actors and a live audience. It has to be staged. You have to reset your compass. Almost learn a new language.

There was a time when I had the idea for a play and no knowledge or experience of how to go about it. I could write a book at that point, but I couldn't write a play. Only exposure to that world, and a few more years of writing experience, gave me the wherewithal to even attempt a theatrical piece.

And, even then, only when we had actually produced and performed the play could I finally sit back and say 'yes, I pulled it off'. Until then, it was still a complete shot in the dark.

I found that I'd learned a new language.

The same with film. It's different again. It's a story told with pictures. Yes, I know it has dialogue and characters too, but it's not called the motion-picture industry for nothing. It's another language. And you have to learn it.

You can bring your transferable skills along with you as you move between different formats and media. And being multi-skilled increases your chances of success.

You can adapt your own books. You can produce your own plays. You can dream of seeing your work on the big or small screen.

You're multi-lingual, multi-talented, and you can get your stories to your audience in a variety of ways. Doesn't sound too bad, does it? So let's go do it.

SCREENWRITING.
PART ONE

Okay. We're going to do this in three parts, for the simple reason that it's an area that I have some experience in, and also because I find it fascinating, interesting, and fun. That's three parts right there. But also because screenplays have a beginning, middle, and end. And screenplays are all about structure.

When I did my Master's degree in Writing, part of my reason for doing so was because I wanted, one day, to teach the Screenwriting Master's. Yet I would only allow myself to do so, if I had earned my credentials on screen. I didn't want to be up there spouting 'theory'. I wanted to be able to say, 'this might not be the way to go about writing scripts, but it's my way, and it works'.

As I'm still awaiting the credentials to be able to say that, this is a taste of the screenwriting course that lies in that unknown future.

How do you write a screenplay? Well, if you're unfamiliar with the layout, look up a movie screenplay online. Much like a play, they are presented in a very particular format.

Unlike a novel or a book, where words form sentences and then paragraphs and then pages, and chapters, on and on until the end, a play or screenplay demands certain things from you: that description should run from side to side on the page, just like a book, but that character's names must be centred on the page, and their dialogue indented.

The layout you can learn in a minute, but creating a screenplay that actually makes it into the multiplexes might take you a lifetime.

Why is that? Well, because films cost money. You face more of a challenge creating a winning script than you do when you try to create a winning novel, because they just cost so much more to produce.

You still have to wow your audience. You still have to create that work of near-genius. And then you have to find someone who is willing to put one, ten, or even a hundred million pounds or dollars into making it.

And why should they gamble their hard-earned money on bringing your vision to the screen? If someone came up to you and said, 'my life has been amazing. It would make a great book,' would you give them a million pounds to write it?

No way, I hear you say. And films cost more money to make than books. A lot more.

But the multiplexes are there, and they need product. The terrestrial TV stations are there, and they need the same. They need shows, or series, or one-off dramas. And then there is the growing list of streaming services, all desperate to have the latest or the best television series or film.

It's all product, and it has to come from somewhere. And where does it come from? Us. *Writers*.

That's right. You heard it here first. You are that important in the food chain. Do you feel invigorated? Do you feel like writing? I bet you do.

The statement above is actually slightly disingenuous. Producers also play a massive part, and many projects are inspired by their talent, vision, and financing, with the writer only brought on board at the appropriate hour. The important thing to know is that you will be in there somewhere, either as the instigator or as a pen for hire.

Again, it's another craft to learn, and one of the foremost things to mention is that screenplays are structure. I know that there are exceptions to every rule, but you have to know – and to have mastered – the rules, before you can even begin to think about ignoring or breaking them.

How do you go about learning the rules of screenwriting? Well, you buy a book on the subject. (Hey, you already did!). You read sample scripts. Many are available online, or can be ordered, or are sitting in your local bookstore or library.

Grab one, especially one from a film that you know and maybe even love. See how the words appear on the page. Notice the layout. Can you visualise the script coming alive in the hands of actors?

If you ever get the opportunity, once you have a script of suitable merit, try and get a bunch of actors (amateurs will do) to read your script aloud. You'll learn a bunch of things. Does it sound real, interesting, and funny in all of the right places?

Ultimately, that's what you'll be asking your script to do: come off the page and take on a life of its own, but it's your responsibility in the first place to put that life in there so that it can be found. It needs to inspire everyone who reads it. Your passion for the story, and your talent to deliver it, need to shine out. Hopefully, it will be glaringly obvious, in all of its glory, right there on the page, so that actors, directors, and producers can work with it and ultimately deliver it to an audience.

For about three years, I was a member of the London Screenwriter's Workshop. I went on to write about ten speculative scripts, all feature-length, because I had a passion for film. One of these was eventually optioned. I currently have a major screenplay project underway. It might never come to fruition, but it's still a writing journey and I'm still improving my craft.

With two friends, I once wrote a ten-minute short script and then we filmed it. I wanted a producer credit. My mate wanted to direct. The other person wanted to act. We came together and made it happen. We got another friend to come up with an original song for the soundtrack. We shot a few scenes in a bar borrowed from someone else that we knew. Ultimately, we made a short movie. It hasn't done anything, but it did a lot for us. We all got to live out our dreams. My printed words made it onto the screen.

So, how do you write a screenplay? How do you get a total stranger to invest millions of pounds in your creation? Well, you have to deliver *a story that will work as a film*. That means it has to have parts in it that actors want to play. It has to have challenges. You can't just say 'This is Joe. He wants to climb Everest. Oh, there he is at the top, planting his flag.'

His wife and children need to beg him not to go. But why doesn't he listen to their earnest pleas? Why does he go anyway? Was it a promise made to someone? Some back-story. A childhood incident concerning his father? It can't just be selfish. Ultimately, your main character is the *hero* of the story. And he can't just achieve it without overcoming a series of obstacles. The more serious and intimidating, the better. In this case, it's Everest. Your guy, he's going to lose his grip at some point. Frostbite is setting in. And then there's an avalanche. And then his best friend falls at the last moment. It can't be easy. *Drama is conflict*. Remember that.

I didn't say it. The experts did. And they're right.

One of the very best books on screenwriting (and there are several good ones) is William Goldman's *Adventures in the Screen Trade*. After giving great background knowledge to all of the films he's written, and been involved with (*Marathon Man* and *Butch Cassidy and the Sundance Kid* to name a couple), he leaves readers with two over-riding statements when it comes to writing screenplays.

Nobody Knows Anything, by which he means that Hollywood and the movie industry never knows what will work and what will not.

That crazy idea you have? Might not be so crazy after all. I've been editing a script lately for someone with no experience in the business. Their story makes me say 'no, no, no' at every turn. But, guess what, it is just so wrong that it might be right. I've never heard the likes of it. Maybe no-one else has either.

For example, Neil Jordan, writer and director, pitched *The Crying Game* to film producers and met the following response.

Neil - It's about a bloke who works for the IRA.

Producer - I don't like that.

Neil – The bloke fails in the mission that the IRA gives him.

Producer - I don't like that.

Neil - He takes a message (a dying wish from the bloke that he is meant to kill) to a hairdresser.

Producer - I'm underwhelmed by that.

Neil - The female hairdresser turns out to be a man!

Producer - I *really* don't like that.

And then the producer said, 'I didn't like any of those individual things, but overall, I like it!'

By the way, Neil Jordan is an amazing writer. The word 'genius' springs to mind. Check out his novels. That's one bloke right there who can move effortlessly between literature and film.

But nobody knows anything. No-one knows what will work and what won't. That's why the film industry is obsessed with sequels. They are seen as a safe pair of hands. They have brand-awareness and a built-in audience. Even if only half the people who saw the original tune in for part two, that's still a safer bet than an unknown quantity.

It's worth saying again. *No-one knows anything.*

William Goldman's other famous maxim is that *Screenplays are structure*.

So what does he mean by that? Well, that's why there's a part two.

SCREENWRITING. PART TWO

So you've got a great idea for a movie, something that you think would work well on the silver screen. What's it about?

That's right. Can you tell me about it in a sentence? Imagine if you invited a friend, or a date, or your partner, to go to the movies to go see a film. What would their response be?

The first thing they would ask you is, 'What's it about?'

Say you were to answer, 'It's about a man and a machine that get sent back in time to try and change a future that hasn't happened yet.'

Assuming they're still interested, the next thing they would ask you is 'Who's in it?'

After all, if they are going to be enticed by your offer, it must have a hook and, where films are concerned, that generally boils down to the story and the cast.

So, your movie must be *about* something, and it must also have suitably interesting characters to attract the attention of good actors.

Generally, your movie will be about someone, who wants something, but who can't easily get it because something stands in their way. Overcoming the obstacles in order to achieve their goal is what your movie is ultimately about.

A feature-length film will generally have a three-act structure. Essentially, this is your beginning, middle, and end.

Act One will be where you introduce us to the main character. We'll find out where we are in the world and when, e.g., are we in Paris in the 1800s, or in New York in the 1980s, or in London, England, in the present day? We'll meet the main character and we'll see them in their ordinary world surroundings.

We'll meet their friends or family, and we'll find out about their specific goal. What is it that they want? What is it that we're going to spend the rest of the movie watching them trying to achieve?

You must, and I mean *must*, establish your central character and their goal and their ordinary world within the first ten minutes of your movie.

Don't believe me? Go watch a film. Stop reading this book right now and go choose a movie from your DVD collection and put it on. Watch the first ten minutes.

Then stop the film.

Do you know who the main character is?

Do you know what their ordinary world is, (i.e., where they are and when), and their own particular circumstances, (e.g., rich, poor, single parent, escaped convict, etc.)?

Do you know what they want?

If you can answer yes to all three questions, then you can bet that it's a pretty good film.

That's your first ten minutes.

Say we are talking about a two-hour movie, you'll be looking to create a 120-page script. One page of correctly formatted screenplay equates to one minute of time on film. Your three-act script, therefore, means you have about 30 minutes for Act One, 60 minutes of conflict for Act Two, and 30 minutes of tortured resolution for Act Three.

You know what you have to achieve in the first ten minutes, so what happens between then and the end of Act One? Well, you can introduce your supporting characters, tell a few jokes, let us meet a few more of their associates, and move us towards what we believe to be the main character's goal.

Then, whammy!

The end of Act One will be your first plot point.

Here, something happens that takes the story in a completely new direction. You thought your movie was about so-and-so wanting this, but now it's about something else entirely. Act One is over, baby.

Now comes Act Two, and it's a completely different ball game. I never knew I was watching a movie about *this*!

Ever seen Thelma and Louise? Two women want to escape their dreary lives and their partners and take off on a girl's weekend. It's hard enough just getting away. One of them has to sneak out behind the back of her annoying boyfriend.

Eventually, they get in the car and manage to break away. It's a movie about a girl's vacation, right?

They've told us from the off that they really want, and need, this trip. They've earned it, and we've watched them for the first ten minutes doing everything they need to, just to get to the point where they can start the car and set off on their journey.

We know our characters. We know where we are (America in the 80s), and we know the situation. Two women, trying to get a break from their partners. And all in the first ten minutes. That's a good movie. As an audience, at this point, we're involved and we're going along for the ride.

The rest of Act One sees the girls chatting away as they set out on the road and starting to have a little fun before they eventually make a pit-stop. And things go quickly sour. Someone gets a little too friendly with one of our girls. Some bloke tries to take advantage, won't take no for an answer, and is now on the verge of committing a heinous act. Until the other woman shoots him. Dead. Now the girls are on the run.

That's your first plot point right there: the moment where the movie spins on its head and goes off in a completely different direction.

Thought you were watching a movie about two women going on a holiday? Well, now you're watching a movie about two women on the run.

Act Two is where you place most of your obstacles to your character or characters achieving their goal.

Put simply, your three-act structure is this: you take your character and you put them up a tree. Then you throw rocks at them. And then you bring them back down again. That's your three-act structure. That's your movie in a nutshell.

The middle or second act, which we are straight into after our first plot point, is all of the resistance that we meet as we attempt to achieve our goal. This is where we throw those rocks at our character while he's stuck up that tree. This is where we lose our money, our job, our girlfriend. The car breaks down. The trains go on strike. The whole world, the fates, are all conspiring to frustrate our ambitions.

Drama is conflict, and it's here in Act Two where your conflict resides.

Remember this, second act trauma makes for third act magic.

After 60 minutes of madness and mayhem, we make the transition into Act Three with the second of our plot points. The goal changes once again. Instead of just wanting to win whatever it was that we wanted to win, we've realised that the prize was really a placebo all along. Unless our main character changes and grows, the prize will ultimately be meaningless. Really, what we want is something that we didn't realise we needed, but that has been our secret yearning all along.

Now that we know what we *really* want, it becomes more important than ever that we get it. But we're not out of the woods yet. That baddie still needs killing. The road back to where we started, even though we'll arrive there as a changed and better person, is still full of potholes. And we've still got 30 minutes' worth of screen-time to fill before we get there.

Act Three is where you see the goal ripped from your grasp, even though you're so close, and even though the prize means everything to you, now that you know what it is that you've really been looking for all of your life. You can't just have it. That would be cheap and a betrayal to your audience who have invested so much time and interest in your story.

Want to travel around the world in 80 days? Boy, you were so close, but you didn't make it, even though you've traversed the entire planet and overcome every obstacle to try and get there, but you just missed out.

Or did you?

Remember that international date-line that you crossed back when? That means it's not today, it's still yesterday! You can still make it if you run quickly. And so you run. And your character runs. And the whole audience runs with you.

Finally, you burst through the doors of the Reform Club in London with only a few seconds to spare and, to the relief of everyone, you declare yourself the victor.

Prize won. Movie over. Audience happy.

There you have it. A two-hour movie, told in three acts, featuring two plot points, and a beginning, middle, and end.

What's it about? And who's in it? That's all people really want to know.

Tell an interesting story, complete with unexpected twists and turns, and make your characters the kind that quality actors will want to play.

Remember, movies cost money. Lots of it. No one is going to stump up that kind of cash unless your script and your story are worth it, and also that you can attract good actors to be in it.

The great news is – if you want to be a screenwriter – your homework is simply to watch movies.

Go and enjoy some of your 10,000 hours. Identify the main character. Recognise their ordinary world. Try to understand what they want. Then, as you become more proficient, try to identify the breaks between the acts, incited by plot points one and two.

If you're serious about the craft of screenwriting, try and take yourself to the cinema at least once a month. Watch films on the big screen as well as at home. It's a different experience, watching a film amongst a paying audience, and one that will probably make you appreciate your craft even more. It should also serve to inspire you. After all, that's where you want to be, with your name on the big screen.

As the credits appear, imagine your name up there.

And your role? Screenwriter.

SCREENWRITING. PART THREE

As we've been talking about a three-act structure for your screenplay, I think it's only right that we should have a screenwriting part three. A beginning, middle, and end.

When you come to write your script, you must visualise what you want your audience to see on the screen and then simply (Ha!) transcribe it.

The first thing you have to do, at the outset of every single scene, is tell us three things.

Firstly, is this an internal or an external shot, i.e., are we indoors or outdoors?

Then, tell us where we are, i.e., the location.

Lastly, tell us if it is day or night.

To be clear, *every* scene that you ever write must begin in this way.

It's a kind of shorthand that sets the scene and avoids any confusion between writer and reader. You set it out it like this.

INT. BAR. NIGHT.

Or:

EXT. FARM. DAY.

Or:

INT. SPACESHIP. DAY.

Or:

EXT. ROADSIDE. NIGHT.

That's enough information to headline the scene. Now, you have to expand a little on that heading.

For the first of the scenes above, you might open with a paragraph that says:

INT. BAR. NIGHT.

Inside a modern, well-lit bar, lots of cool young people are busy chatting and drinking with their friends.
Music is playing. Lights are flashing. It's a happening environment. Busy.

Into the bar walks KATE, a beautiful young woman, dressed to impress.

You use your prose to expand your description and give the reader a bit more information.

Following a short description to describe the surroundings, giving just enough information to set the scene, you will then introduce your characters, and then they will start to speak to each other using witty, sharp, imaginative, or thought-provoking and interesting language.

Within that dialogue will be the representation of their hopes and dreams, and the information that you need to share with an audience.

Necessary information given within the dialogue is known as exposition, as it 'exposes' certain facts that you want your viewers to be aware of.

The novice writer does clunky exposition. The smart writer finds other ways to get that information across without being too obvious. Challenge yourself to try to stay ahead of your audience and not bore them when serving up your exposition.

Imagine your movie is an old-style Western. If you have two characters, and one of them says to the other 'how long is it that you've been on the run, Butch?' – well that could be described as obvious exposition. We now know that Butch is on the run because the other character came right out and said it.

But what if you had Butch looking furtively out of the window, and then the camera cuts away to a wanted poster that's been torn off a wall and now lies on the dressing room table. We would still know that Butch is a wanted man, but no-one came right out and said it. The clever and experienced writer found another way.

Here's how the scenario above might look in screenplay format.

INT. LOG CABIN. DAY.

Two men sit inside a sparse hut. They are both in their mid-thirties. Gruff, worn. They've seen a lot of life.

One of them is loading bullets into a revolver. The other stares furtively out of the window, checking the coast is clear. On the dressing table is a wanted poster, torn down from its previous post.

It shows a man with a £10,000 dollar bounty on his head. Wanted, dead or alive. His name is BUTCH. He's one of the two men currently in residence in the log cabin.

When the two characters start to speak, it will look like this on the page.

Let's call his partner Sundance for now.

              SUNDANCE
        You got enough ammo?

                BUTCH
    There's no such thing as enough.

              SUNDANCE
    That's right. We don't know how many men we gotta kill today. See anyone?
                BUTCH
    Not yet. But they're out there somewhere.

Sundance puts his gun in a holster and gets to his feet.

Butch does the same.

Get the picture?
Okay, I'm not winning any Oscars for that lot, but hopefully it's given you a feeling for what your story should look like in screenplay form.

You have your scene heading (INT/EXT, etc.) followed by a brief description of the place and the people in it, and then you centre the character's name when they're speaking, and indent the dialogue afterwards so that it's easier for your actors or your prospective producer to find and read. That's your script layout. There's really no more to the actual layout than that.

Your screenplay will be made up of maybe 30 or 40 short scenes. Each scene should last roughly three or four minutes. What you end up with is a script of about 100 to 120 pages, which is about an hour fifty or two hours of screen-time.

That's a movie.

Your scenes can develop a momentum of their own. When scenes run into each other or form a block of action, that becomes known as a sequence, but it will still be made up of individual scenes.

You may have a main plot and one or two sub-plots. Take a film like *On The Waterfront*. What's it about? Well, you could say it's about corruption in America's docklands, but isn't it also a story about an ex-boxer and the good girl that he falls in love with?

A good movie will interweave the different strands, floating effortlessly between its main plot and the one or two sub-plots. You can use one to take a break from the other. Your sub-plot might be a good place to introduce some humour to the story or a theme that concerns another of your characters.

So, now you know how to present your screenplay in the appropriate format. You know how it should be laid out on the page. Your succession of scenes – like pearls on a necklace – form your feature-length screenplay.

The more you write, the better you will get. The more you know about the rules, the better you will be able to bend or break them to keep your writing fresh and original.

A screenplay should come in at around 25,000 words, so about a quarter or a third of the size of your average novel. That means you should be able to write three or four screenplays in the same time as it would take you to write one book.

If a book is going to take you a year to write, see if you can't knock out a screenplay in three or four months.

Another great tip from the master, William Goldman, is to write that script as fast as you can. If it's going to take you two years to write, then you're a different person by the time you finish than you were at the start.

That's not good. How can you remain consistent? Write fast. Don't start until you're ready but, as soon as you are, write as fast as you can. An added bonus is that some of that energy will transfer itself onto the page.

Don't worry about making mistakes. You can always go back and correct those later on. Rewriting is writing, they say, and especially so in screenwriting.

Budd Schulberg, Oscar-winning screenwriter of *On the Waterfront* gave the following advice: always keep moving and always aim for the end. Those are the words of a master, and are probably the two things your story needs to achieve. Is there action? Are we going somewhere? If you're floundering around, instead of getting to the point of the story, your audience will grow bored and you will lose them.

In fact, you're unlikely to even *get* an audience, as no one is going to make your movie anyway. If your script doesn't grab the people with the power to make it, then how are they going to believe that the finished product will grab anybody else?

That said, bad movies do get made. You can learn as much by watching them as you can by watching the good ones. But try and write the best that you can. You'll be following in the footsteps of some of the greatest writers of all time, including playwrights and novelists, who all put their work up on the silver screen.

Be a writer. Be a screenwriter. And always be the best that you can be.

THE DIFFERENCE BETWEEN FILM AND TV WRITING

If you compare a TV script to a film script, the layout would look pretty similar. So what's the difference between writing for TV and for film?

I'll be honest, I have no great background in TV writing, though I have submitted scripts to the BBC and had them commended by their Writers Room service (a site you should check out and keep in touch with online). I've also been queue-jumped for future projects on the strength of a sample script.

I can only tell you what I *think* is the difference based on 30 years of studying the craft, my Master's degree in Writing, and what I have read and learned from others with experience in these fields.

The difference between film and television is probably best answered by yourself. If you think you are going to watch a film at the cinema, what are you expecting to see? The answer is probably something epic. Something out of the ordinary. Films deal with the extraordinary world. They are larger than life.

When you sit down in front of the TV at the end of your working day, do you expect to have the same experience? I would guess not. You expect to experience the everyday stuff. People chatting in a bar or a shop. Their everyday existence reflecting your own. This is the very prose of life. The simple struggle in getting from A to B. The highs and lows of an ordinary existence.

Imagine if they made a movie of *Coronation Street*. Would it simply be three episodes of Corrie stuck together, or would you expect something a bit different? Maybe something more?

Of course you would, because movies are just *bigger*.

I realise, of course, that these comments are in danger of rapidly becoming (and may already be) outdated. TV is now *the* place to be. It is no longer the kid brother to film. It can now hold its own with, and even outdo, its grander sibling.

Most of the explanations given in this chapter are hypothetical. Essentially, film is a cinematic language, one told through the medium of pictures as well as language. TV is a medium where language takes precedence over the visual aspect. The language in the latter usually contains a lot more exposition than we would see or hear in a film.

I would say that the use of more down to earth language, more expositionary (i.e., obvious) dialogue is the first real difference when it comes to writing for these two different media.

The second difference is that a film should be a more cinematic experience. It should play better on the big screen. In terms of scale, film is big, and television is small, (although that landscape is changing all the time). You can now deliver epic on the small screen too.

Finally, you need to think about the length of the piece you are writing. Films are usually one-off pieces. You must tell us everything in your two hours (or thereabouts) and leave no loose ends at the finale of the piece. If you're writing for a weekly soap or a serial drama, then you need to sustain the audience's interest over weeks, months, and maybe even years.

You need to incorporate cliff-hangers at the end of every episode, and before commercial breaks to ensure that people tune in next week or after the ad-break. But it's all writing, it's all story, and it all involves characters interacting with each other as they go about their business.

In a film, you are probably going to concentrate on one central character, on *what it is* that they want, and the obstacles that get in the way of them achieving their goal. In a TV drama, you may be writing for multiple people. You may have storylines A, B, and C to juggle on a weekly basis.

But we can do it. Right?

Television is a growing force in the field of entertainment. Producers and networks are crying out for great writers. At the end of the day, we are still just storytellers, in whichever medium we happen to be working. We have to practice our craft, deliver, and astound. Otherwise, how are you ever going to stand out from the crowd?

While the differences between writing for either TV or film may appear quite subtle, yet important, series like *Breaking Bad*, *The Sopranos*, and *Game of Thrones*, (to name just a few), have put TV on a par with their feature film counterparts. You can now write 'big' for the small screen too.

One way to break into either is to write that spec, meaning speculative, script. This means that no-one is paying you to write it, and no one is specifically waiting on the other end to receive it.

Agents and producers may declare that they aren't taking any unsolicited submissions. In that case, you'll have to think outside of the box to find someone who *is* accepting submissions at the present time. And then you wait.

The BBC has its own Writers Room service which accepts submissions on a (usually) once-a-year basis. Write a script that shows them your talent. They might not produce that particular script, but they may want to see more of your stuff. They could even steer you towards one of their mentoring programmes, and get you to write an episode for one of their daytime dramas. You'll then have your foot in the door. Your audience will await. And you'll have the Beeb, or Channel Four, or whichever network takes you on, giving you the encouragement and nurturing that you need.

I know that's exactly what I'm going to do. I've asked myself, what television dramas do I like? Which have been my all-time favourites, including those from my childhood? What would I like to contribute to the canon of that work?

I've come up with an idea. It will be one-hour long, i.e., 60 minutes and therefore 60 pages of script. It will showcase my work and hopefully my talent. Once the deadline passes and the submission window has closed, somewhere inside the BBC will be my calling-card script.

Then I'll wait. It's still a lottery, but you know what they say about those. In order to be in with a chance of winning, you've got to buy a ticket. Or, in our case, write a script.

Don't ever aim to write for a series or soap that you don't like or even love. Write something that you feel passionate about. That passion – believe me – will be picked up on by your reader. These people aren't stupid. They're production executives, script supervisors, and story editors, and they all love a good story.

Make sure that you floor them with yours. Try to write to the best of your ability. You may have to wait a further year for the next opening or opportunity, so make sure that you seize your chance. Good luck. And that goes for all of us.

HOW TO ADAPT A BOOK

Say you've read a book, or written one, and you want to adapt it for a different medium, like radio, or theatre, or film. How do you go about that?

Well, the first thing you have to do, if you're planning this as a commercial venture (i.e., not just writing it for your own practice), is address any copyright issues.

If it's your own work that you're adapting, or the work of a writer who has been dead for more than seventy years (which is the usual expiry of copyright), then you can just go ahead and write your adaptation. If you want to use someone else's work, say an adaptation of a current bestselling book or just a novel that you love, then you need to find out who owns the rights and try to broker a deal. It's complicated, and you should look the matter up in greater detail than I'm planning to include here.

Assuming there are no copyright issues, how do you go about adapting an existing work for a whole different medium?

Probably the most important thing to say is that your destination is key. What are you planning to turn it into?

I have written and produced stage versions of *Frankenstein*, *Great Expectations*, and *A Christmas Carol*. These are all famous works, yet none are subject to any copyright restrictions, due to the time that has passed since their authors' demise.

That said, I've also produced works that were subject to copyright restrictions. A bit of research, and a well-written letter still got me through the door and gave me the access I needed to produce both a play and a book on the life of Tommy Cooper, and also to utilise Fenton Bresler's book about the murder of John Lennon for my play *One Bad Thing*.

Even if the original work of literature is long out of copyright, you can still fall foul of other people's later adaptations. Better to write your own. One Hollywood studio claims the copyright for the image of Frankenstein's monster. Want two bolts in your monster's neck and a large forehead? Forget it! They own it. Just dispense with their version and summon up a monster of your own, and then you're good to go.

Go to the source material, and take from that what you need to tell the story that you wish to tell.

Ultimately, you can't be too wedded to the original. You don't want to deliver a bad play or movie from a great book, just because you had too much respect for the source material. You can't make an omelette without breaking eggs. You have to break it down and then build it back up again. It's a transformer. Theirs was a great-looking book. Yours is a great-looking play.

You can't have too much reverence for the original material. You have to take it in your hands as if it were a piece of clay. Scrunch it up in your hands. All of those characters, that story, all of that dialogue, they're all still there in that rolled-up ball of clay. Now you have to fashion a different shape out of it because you're adapting it for a different medium.

And, because a book is usually so many words longer than those needed for a theatre or film script, you're going to leave at least half of that ball of clay on a shelf in your writing room. It's a shame – a crying shame – but you can't just re-write the book. It has to work as something else.

Get to the essence of the story. Take only as many characters with you as you can afford to carry on that journey. You have to travel light. Lighter than the book.

Keep what you need. Do you really need those night-vision goggles, that camping stove, that spare sleeping bag? You're going to have to be a lean, mean, marching machine. Take what you need and nothing more. Well, maybe a little more. You can allow yourself the odd indulgence, but you can't take it all. Otherwise, that's still the book. It's not an adaptation.

Do you want to know what works particularly well in adaptation? A short story. Stephen King once wrote a book called *Different Seasons*, containing four short stories or novellas (short novels). Each was about 25,000 words in length. Three of them have been turned into movies. They were *Stand By Me*, *The Shawshank Redemption*, and *Apt Pupil*. The last of the four novellas, entitled *The Breathing Method*, is slated for film production in 2020.

Now we're talking about a master writer here. There'll be very little fat in those stories, and therefore very little that has to be removed. And 25,000 words is about the same amount that you would find in a feature-length film script. In a scenario such as this, there's no need to abandon much of the text. You can pretty much use it all. Each vessel is the same size. Pour the contents of one into the other. Novella into film.

A short story is basically anything between 1,000 and 25,000 words. A novella is between 25,000 and 50,000 words. Anything over 50,000 is a novel. Anything over, say, 200,000 words is a long novel, or even a work of literature. So now you know.

Back to adaptations. Remember, if it was a great book, it will still be a great book, no matter what you create in another medium. (That said, hang your head in shame if you should deliver something so empty it puts people off reading the classic version!)

Your job when adapting a book is to create a great play or a great film from the source material. In order to do that, remember that you are still – first and foremost – writing a play or a film. The book is history, as far as you're concerned.

Read the source material, get it under your skin, and then write a great play or a great film.

Try and pick up a cheap copy of the original book. Go through it with a highlighter pen and mark every bit of action or dialogue that you want to include. Try and stay faithful to the text, but don't be afraid to leap, gazelle-like, over huge tracts of it to get to the next beat in your story, your version, of their original work.

This is your film, or your play. You'll do a disservice to the original, and to the people who love that source material (of which you're probably one) if you don't deliver a brilliant adaptation. This is *your* version of *their* work. Go do them proud.

OTHER AVENUES

I feel qualified to talk about writing plays, books, and screenplays. I've written and produced eight of the former, of which four were original pieces and four were adaptations. I've also written and published seven books, of which two were fiction and five were non-fiction. I've gathered three book publishing deals along the way and I've had a Daily Mail book of the week in 2019. I've written about a dozen spec screenplays, one of which has been optioned, and one of which is in development. This stuff I know.

But what about other avenues for writing? What if you want to follow a route that we haven't yet covered and which, to be honest, I'm probably not really qualified to teach?

The best thing I can say is this. Within the pages of this book, you will find inspiration. We'll soon talk about your writing day, how to get an agent, how to get published, and other facets of the writing world. If you wish to specialise, however, in an area that I have no expertise in, then I think it would be disingenuous of me to pretend otherwise and to waffle on for the sake of it.

Instead, I propose to discuss what those other avenues might be, and then encourage you to go and find the resources you need to learn about these subjects and tackle whatever obstacles you may find in your way. I already know how determined you are. After all, you've come this far already. So, I guess you really do want to be a writer.

You may wish to write a kids book. How do you go about that? I can only say that I would urge you to read a lot of them and try to get a feel for the genre. David Walliams is enjoying huge success in this field at the moment. He is seemingly the heir-apparent to Roald Dahl.

Books such as *The Gruffalo* have also risen to the top of the pile, finding favour with children across the globe.

And what about perennial favourites such as Aesop's fables or The Brother's Grimm? These books are full of great characters and timeless stories, whilst also containing a deeper message that touches a nerve in the subconscious of children and older readers alike. *Little Red Riding Hood*, for example, is a timeless warning not to take things at face value and to always be on your guard, especially in the company of strangers.

Master the genre, practice it yourself by producing your own work, and gain feedback in order to improve. Your first readers can be your friends. When you've convinced them that you know what you're doing, place your text in the hands of professionals. See what reaction you get there. Keep writing. Keep improving.

The same applies if you want to write crime fiction. It's hard to do unless you're an aficionado of the field. Learn the rules. Master them. Then write your own. Get it read by others. Absorb your readers' comments. Go for the jugular. Wow 'em.

There are so many avenues for your writing. Not just in terms of producing something that you're proud of, but also for earning a living, or for keeping your dream alive of one day striking it rich.

You could try to break into the world of journalism. There, at least, you'll be writing every day. Many fiction and non-fiction writers are former (or continuing) journalists. You'll learn how to hit a deadline. You'll probably have an exciting career. You'll be earning as you write. You can still write that novel or screenplay on the side. And it's an avenue for your writing.

The same goes with being a poet, or writing a radio play, or even wanting to write soaps on television, or scripts for increasingly-layered computer games.

I've written my fair share of poetry, though not for a while. Did performance poetry too, getting up at comedy gigs and doing my thing. I was, I admit, that angry Northern poet ruining your evening of fun. Mostly, it was an exercise in wanting to be heard, waiting for your turn, and paying little attention to the other acts who were hogging the limelight and taking too long on the stage when the real talent, (i.e. me, the sensitive poet), was having to stand in line and wait in the wings.

It was an apprenticeship of sorts, and one that has been served by plenty of writers, but I don't think too many of us spend our whole careers in that field. Not if we expect to do it for a living, anyway.

The BBC air about two radio plays every day. They are relatively inexpensive to produce (at least compared to visual media). You could try your hand at one of those, with words that leap off the page. It's a true storytelling art form.

Similarly, if you love the soaps, knock on their door. Submit a piece of writing. Put on a rehearsed reading of a script at a venue and invite everyone you know, and anyone in the industry that you can think of, to come along and hear your work.

I know a scriptwriter for Corrie who got her break by putting on a play in Edinburgh. Someone connected to our longest-running soap saw the show, knew they had an opening on the writing team, and the rest was a lucrative contract with her work performed to about ten million people every week.

Not bad work if you can get it. Not bad money either.

One of my actors, a fine fellow, got an acting gig for a big computer game. Nowadays, they use real actors in the parts so that they can create realistic graphics. The first game he appeared in became a huge global hit. By the time they made the second in the series, he was being shot by numerous cameras flying 360 degrees around him. The production values were off the scale. Then, when Hollywood saw the money these games were generating (I'm talking blockbuster film-type revenue), they also started to pour money into the franchise and into the industry as a whole.

The audience for these games is also growing more sophisticated. These aren't just shoot-em-ups they're creating anymore. Now, they want real stories to go with the images and the manoeuvrability. And who creates stories? We do. The writers.

Love computer games? Go write one, or approach the people and companies that make them and ask if they have an opening in their storytelling department.

Not hard, is it? Look them up online, or on the back of the box the game came in. Send them an email, or write them a letter, or give them a call.

If you have a literary CV, send them a copy. All you've got to say is 'Hello. I'm a writer. Got any openings for a writer?'

What could be easier? You never know, they might just say yes.

In fact, they might be scratching their heads at the very moment that you make contact, wondering how they can move their enterprise forward. You could be the answer to their prayers. And they could be the answer to yours.

I would say that, whatever avenue you choose to pursue, you should have a passion for the genre, just as much as you have a passion for whatever story it is that you wish to share.

It's not easy foregoing time you could be spending with friends and loved ones to plonk your backside on a chair and fill an empty page, or even a thousand of them. Love your genre. Love your story. And write.

And just because you enjoy some success in one particular field, it doesn't mean that you're stuck in that paddock forever. Hop over the fence. Tell your story in the medium best-suited to the tale. Amaze others. Amaze yourself. Stories know no boundaries. Neither should you.

WRITING FOR TELEVISION

We've touched on this subject already, but I don't think that we're quite done yet. Most of us have a TV in the home. Most of us watch it from time to time, or even every day. There, right in front of you, literally staring you in the face, is a possible source of income for your writing and an outlet for your talent as a storyteller.

Both the BBC and Channel 4 run regular (by which I mean at least once a year) searches for new writers. There are opportunities to submit sample scripts. They can be, literally, about anything at all. The only criteria that your spec script must meet is that you must show some understanding of the medium.

Now the medium itself is not hard to understand. We all (or most of us, anyway) watch TV. But that's not what I'm talking about. By an understanding of the medium, I mean an understanding of *writing* for the medium. The best way to do that is to carefully read the submission guidelines that will accompany the opportunity.

Essentially, the people reading your script, and the hundreds (if not thousands) of other scripts that they receive every year, want some sort of level playing field so that they can judge us all on a similar basis.

If someone submits a five-minute comedy sketch, and someone else submits a two-hour drama, they can't really compare those two scripts on a like-for-like basis. So, what they want is a 30 minute or, even better, a 60 or 90-minute sample of your writing. In a complete script, they can better judge how you can hold all of the elements together. Does your main character grow and change throughout their journey? Are the various story strands brought to a satisfactory conclusion? Can you maintain the drama for the duration of the piece?

Can you write interesting characters? How strong is your main story? How relevant, amusing, and divergent are the sub-plots? How realistic or witty is your dialogue? Basically, can you write?

You don't have a lot of time to hook your audience, and don't forget that your first audience is the reader who is judging your work. Keep it interesting. What, exactly, is at stake for your main character, your protagonist? You need to let your reader know what that is, and you also have to make them care about it.

Ever seen the film The Full Monty? If you have, you'd probably say that it's a film about a group of men who become male-strippers. If you were to ask the actors what their motivations were, they would comment that it's about a group of desperate, unemployed, financially-stricken blokes who resort to the unthinkable in order to escape their situation. And if you asked Robert Carlyle, the main character, what it's about, he would respond (as he has in several interviews) that it's about an estranged father wanting to re-connect with his son. Layers upon layers.

So you have a character or characters. They have their everyday world. They want to somehow change it for the better. You have to set up the obstacles in the way of them achieving their goal. You need to convince your first reader to stay glued to the page. If you can do that, then they can hopefully envisage the viewer, ultimately, being glued to the screen, whenever the piece is eventually filmed and released.

Remember, if this is a commercial network, (and I suppose even the BBC is a commercial network as it has to justify its licence fee), they want to know that advertisers will tie their colours to the mast of your production. So, you've got to wow your reader, who is essentially the gatekeeper to your eventual viewer.

How do you write good characters?

One of the best ways that I've ever heard it described, is this. Write a character, and you will have created a type. Create a type, and you will have created nothing at all.

If you put your imagination and your heart and soul into creating a fictional character, dreamt up by yourself, your audience will still find themselves saying, 'Oh, he's an eccentric, or he's a miser, or a bully, or a charmer'.

Whatever it is that your unique character is, people will still identify him as a type.

Take Victor Meldrew. Even though we'd rarely seen his like on TV before, and even though he was brilliantly written and superbly acted, he's still a grumpy old sod in the minds of your audience. You wrote a character. The audience identified him as a type.

Imagine, then, if you tried to take a short-cut. You wanted to get on with telling your main story. You were too focussed on the main character to bother sketching out the other people playing alongside him (or her). Instead of going to the trouble of creating someone unique, you just outlined a type instead.

You've written a one-dimensional character who is just going to say grumpy stuff. Is that Victor Meldrew? No, it's just someone that we don't know and that we really don't like. By the time the main character comes on to propel your important story along to the next inciting incident, your audience will have wandered off to put the kettle on or – even worse as far as your advertisers are concerned – have turned over completely in search of something better to watch.

Create a character, and you'll find you've created a type. Create a type, and you'll find that you've created nothing at all.

Your script needs a story, characters, and effective dialogue. If you can make your landscape interesting too (like an exotic or unusual setting), so that people enjoy the show, maybe moving between internal and external scenes, then that's all good.

The people reading your script want to be wowed. They want to discover you. They want your voice to be unique. They want to march into their office in the morning and rave about you to their colleagues and superiors. Damn it, they want you in the building writing drama for their schedule.

So what are you waiting for? Go write.

And don't think that your spec script is necessarily going to get made. Out of the thousands of submissions that they will receive, they might find a dozen writers that they want to take a closer look at. Of those, maybe one or two will have actually written something that these broadcasters want to spend the millions on that they cost to produce.

Don't be put off. You might be that one. The point I'm making is that they are searching for talent rather than searching for material.

Let your talent and imagination soar. Write the story you're dying to share with the world. Introduce us to your amazing characters. Wow us with your dialogue. Put your work out there. Because, remember, if you don't buy a lottery ticket, you can't win the prize. And that, ultimately, is why we're here.

THE WRITING DAY

How does your writing day look? How *should* a writing day look? Well, the honest answer is that no two days will ever be exactly the same. That applies whether you are a professional or an aspiring writer. Some of us are morning people, some of us are afternoon or evening people. Some people even write throughout the night.

And what if you don't *have* a writing day. What if you only have a writing hour, or a writing afternoon one day a week?

The important thing to note is that, to be a writer, you need to write. You need to find the time to write as often as possible in order to fulfil your ambition.

Stephen King, in his book *On Writing* says that he told one interviewer, in answer to the question 'How often do you write?', that he writes every day of the year except for Christmas day and his birthday. Then, in his book, he tells us that he'd actually lied to the interviewer. The truth was that he wrote every day, *including* his birthday and Christmas. He couldn't help it. Had to do it. Wanted to do it. Did it anyway.

You should aim for the same.

Now not everyone has the luxury of being able to write every day. We don't have the money in the bank that might allow us to do that, and that's assuming that we even have the desire to write that often.

But I'm going to guess that you do. I know I do. If I could wake up every morning and just go to the computer and write, I'd be a very happy and contented man indeed.

How does your writing day look if you also have a day job? Well, I have one, and I'm about to publish my second book this year. How do I do that? I write for an hour a day, almost every day, when I come home from work.

I set myself a target of 1,000 words. I might write more, I might write less, but at least I have a goal. That hour might be 45 minutes, or it might be an hour and a half. Doesn't matter. I'm writing consistently. There's still some subconscious work going on every time I sit down to write. I have momentum. I have desire. I have a project underway. I'm writing.

Time was, before I was married, whenever I could afford to do so, I'd write for 12 hours a day, unprompted and unpaid, for seven days a week.

I know what you're thinking. That's dedication right there. Or maybe you're just thinking, '*Get a life!*'

The thing is, I did it, and I've done it whenever life has allowed me to do so. Maybe not write to that extent (though don't let me stop you), but write as much and as often as you can. You never know, you might just get rich and famous a little earlier than you hoped or expected.

How did I keep writing for 12 hours a day and for seven days a week?

Well, the seven days a week only happened during occasional periods of unemployment, when either I could afford to take a break or I couldn't find a job. And if I was unemployed, I was skint. And when I say that, I mean as broke as broke can be. Like one of those Parisian artists trading paintings for meals at the local bistro, except no-one wanted my work, so I was even more destitute than that!

My friend, someone who'd grown up in a ghetto, used to say that I was the poorest guy he'd ever met. By that (I hope) he meant the person who had to survive on the least money, and not that I was a poor excuse for a human being!

Whenever I had time on my hands, I would write. Plays, screenplays, novels. Whatever story was next on my list, I wrote it. Once completed, I'd find a way to get it into the hands of publishers, film producers, and anyone I could find in the industry. Nothing would come of them. Still, I'd keep writing with all of the time available to me.

I worked too for most of the time. I've worked my whole life, it seems, yet I've made use of any downtime and written prolifically in that period. If a work contract ended, and I had a little put away in the bank, I'd write until I ran out of money, and then I'd go find another job.

So, back to the question, how can you write for 12 hours a day? The answer is that you can't. Not non-stop, anyway. But here's how you can best go about it.

I'd begin at nine in the morning. I'd write for 90 minutes. Then I'd take a half-hour break. Give my brain a rest.

I'd have a cup of tea. Watch a bit of morning TV. Just switch off and have a cup of tea or coffee, maybe smoke a cigarette or eat a piece of toast or something. Then I'd go back and write for another two hours.

Then I'd break for lunch. I'd give myself a full hour. I'd make myself something to eat, whilst watching more of that daytime TV.

An hour's rest for a brain that is being driven at its maximum. You've got to give it a rest. You've got to learn how to relax and switch off and not tax yourself in those interim moments. After all, you're working hard, right? Give yourself the break you need and that you so richly deserve.

After lunch, do another two hours. Then break for your afternoon coffee. Give yourself half an hour. After all, you'll be feeling the strain by now from all of that endeavour. That connection between what you're thinking and what you're typing comes at a cost. You're working really hard.

Then you do another 90 minutes.

Then you break for dinner. That's a two-hour break. An hour to cook. A half-hour to eat. A half-hour to watch some more of that TV. After that, you spend a couple of hours going over everything you've written; editing, and making changes and improvements.

By now, it's 9pm, and your writing day is done. You've probably got a couple of thousand words down on paper. Those words have been edited too. You're in good shape. Go watch TV, or pop to the pub. Afterwards, go get some sleep, because tomorrow is another writing day.

Write as often as you can. Find a time that suits you.

And write.

WRITING IS A LONELY BUSINESS

Let's not kid ourselves. What we do is odd. Wonderfully odd, I'd like to think, but odd nonetheless.

There are so many other things that we could be doing. Got a family? Got friends? Got a hobby, interests? How do you justify giving any or all of that up to go and sit in a room by yourself and write?

Personally, I think things could be worse. You could be a model-rail enthusiast, spending all of your spare time in your attic with your track and train set. You might enjoy playing video games, and be obsessed with FIFA football, Formula 1, or the latest war game.

I can only say, in defence of us writers, is that the hours we spend alone – writing – have a tangible result. At the end of all of that endeavour, there is a script or a text of some kind.

It may not be publishable or worthy of production. It may be part of your learning or your personal growth. But it exists. What you produce really exists. It was created by you, and you have something to show for your efforts.

How do I justify abandoning my wife for an hour or two each evening, and the same at weekends? I know she would be happier if I was sat next to her on the sofa watching something on TV. It's important to find the time to do just that, but it's equally as important to find the time to write.

Just make sure that the hours that you put aside for writing are productive. Make sure you have something to show for it at the end. After all, you've put everything else to one side to make good on the promise that you made to yourself to write that book, play, or script.

Once you close the door, as you step into your personal writing space, you're on your own. No one is there to crack the whip or to count how many words you've written.

By the way, that's what we writers do. We count words. I know we also write them, but we count them as much as we write them. How many have I written today? Did I reach my target? How many words have I written so far? How many more words do I need to write before my novel, play, or screenplay is complete? That's what we writers do. We count words. You'll only really understand the truth of that when you have a little experience under your belt. When you understand that writers *count* words, you'll probably be well on your way to being an accomplished writer. You'll be getting somewhere.

And as long as you go into your writing space like a person on a mission, that should be all the motivation you need to keep the loneliness at bay.

It comes back to that idea of getting yourself onto a shelf before you take a break. Your shelf is coming up in an hour or in 1,000 words' time anyway, or whatever your specific target is. Try to get as far away from the sound of the TV and from the aromas emanating from the kitchen. Try to forget that your loved one or ones are having fun while you still have work to do.

You have to write. It won't write itself. You've put your hand up and volunteered for the job. Loneliness is just one of the obstacles that you have to face. It's no use feeling sorry for yourself or succumbing to the siren song of the fun that everyone else is having. You've set yourself a task and you have to see it through.

You have to be self-motivated. You have to be disciplined. You have to cherish the idea that you had in the first place, the one that made you say 'This is my next project'. But don't think that anyone is coming to your rescue. Writing is a lonely business.

You could always join a writing group, or undertake a course of study, as I did when I studied for my MA. That makes you a slightly-less lonely writer for as long as it lasts, and for a couple of hours of the week at least. But it won't last forever. Writing is not a sociable activity. It is something that you do alone in a room.

Even if you're lucky enough to get a job writing for a soap opera or a big drama production where they have a team of writers, you'll still have to write on your own.

There will be team meetings, you'll have editorial support, and you will be given direction, but then you'll have to go home and write alone.

The same is true if you get a publishing deal.

You might also get an agent along the way. You'll have a sympathetic voice at the end of the line should you need to make a call. You'll have face-to-face meetings, literary lunches, but all they will ask you is 'How's the book coming along?' They won't help you write it. They'll comment and advise, edit and direct you, but they won't write it for you. That's your job.

Writing is a lonely business. You better get used to that fact.

The good news is, once you've done your hour, or day, or 1,000 words, you get to have fun, or at least relax and do whatever it is that you like to do when you're not writing. Go and blow the dust of that train set. Go watch TV with your wife, or take your kids to the park, or go to the stadium and watch your favourite football team kick a ball around. And hopefully win. In other words. Go live your life.

Writing is work. Work that we love and that we choose to do. No one is holding a gun to our heads. We *choose* to do it because we are *determined* to write.

I've been fortunate. After almost 30 years of writing unprompted and unpaid, I've finally secured several book publishing deals, and I now earn a small income from my writing. When I tear myself away from the company of my wife, I tell her that it's all for a good cause. These royalty cheques pay for our annual holidays.

That's not the reason why I write books, and films, and plays. I simply write stories that I want to share with the world. Nonetheless, while I'm lonely writing, she's lonely watching TV.

Writing is a lonely business, for all of us, by which I mean you and the people around you.

That's just a fact.

But don't let it stop you.

DAYDREAMING. THE BEST PART

For me, daydreaming occupies the space between having the initial idea and carrying out the actual writing.

Say you've come up with that fabulous idea, the one that you're desperate to share with the world. The one that excites you. The only frustrating part is knowing that it might take you six months to get it down in its full form, into its finished state of script, play, or book. But it will come, eventually.

So, you have your idea, and you want to start writing. But you can't. Of course you can't. Because what are you going to say? You've got a long road ahead of you. You need to plan your journey. You also need to make sure that you pack all of your essential ingredients – the tools and provisions that will sustain you in your endeavour – and ensure that you don't flounder along the way.

You need to do the necessary preparation. You need to get in shape. Luckily, we're talking about mental rather than physical preparation here. But you still need to do it.

Imagine if it was an actual physical journey that you were about to embark upon. Say it was a trek across the peaks of the Lake District. You might want to take a rucksack. In it, you'd put your tent and sleeping bag, a few tins of beans, a couple of bottles of water. You'd want a tin opener, maybe a pen-knife. A change of socks. A clean T-shirt. Basically, you're preparing for the journey ahead.

The same with your writing. You've got a great idea for a murder-mystery or a romance novel. You've had that 'what-if' moment. You know it will make a great book.

If you set off immediately, with nothing more than the idea and the belief that it will make a fine novel, you're likely to run out of steam before you make a great deal of headway. You may wander off the path, go round in circles, and end up back at the start feeling dismayed and disillusioned. And why? Because you didn't prepare.

Daydreaming, or free-thinking, is an essential part of the writing process. For me, it's probably my favourite part of the whole process. There's no better feeling than actually writing 'The End', but you should embrace the bit of the journey that is the daydreaming part, because I do believe it is both important and enjoyable.

It might look like you're not doing a lot at this stage. There's nothing to show for your efforts, other than a few notes and bullet-points jotted in your journal. There's no target to complete. You're not writing 1,000 words a day or putting in an hour at the computer. All you're doing is thinking and taking notes. You might be doing this while sat at your favourite beauty spot or staring out the window or even facing out to sea. You may be sat at a quiet table in a café.

And what's so creative about that?

Well, it's here that you can decide who your protagonist is. What sort of a person are they? What sort of a person do you want them to be?

What challenges do you want them to face? Who is the antagonist? What are the obstacles in the way of them achieving their goals? Who are their friends? Who are their enemies?

What other things do you want to say, and who do you want to include?

Put all of these things into your journal. Get creative. Get inventive. Have fun. Think!

Only if you allow yourself the time and space to think about your story, all of its characters, all of its implications, will you be able to properly populate the world that you're about to create.

The subconscious is one of a writer's greatest tools. It will be the engine of your enterprise, the fuel for the journey. Are you going to set off empty? You can't. You need to fill up the tank before you set off on your literary adventure.

Think of your mind as a sponge. You need to soak it with ideas, sub-plots, and footnotes. When you're on your way, you are going to squeeze that sponge whenever you get stuck. You want enough stuff in there so that it can seep out, oiling the wheels, keeping you on track. You don't want to squeeze it and have nothing come out. You'll grind to a halt. Your writing will dry up. You might be halfway through your novel. You'll have wasted months of effort. No one wants or deserves that.

By allowing yourself a week or a month or however long it takes to think freely about your characters, story, and setting, you'll have soaked your sponge. It will be there as your 'go-to' resource when you begin the writing phase.

Because, when you begin writing, immersed you will be. And once you've started, you can't take your sponge back to the well. You need to soak it before you set off. And you do that in the daydreaming phase.

Don't underestimate it. *Do* enjoy it. You're not wasting time, no matter how impatient you might feel to get started with your writing. Better to hold your fire, contemplate all the angles, and consider each relevant point before you embark.

This is a part of your project that you should savour and enjoy. Take a seat on a park bench and watch the world go by, all the while letting your story run through your head. See what comes to mind. What if such and such a character did this? What if so and so were to happen? Play with it. Have fun. There are no limitations here.

Your mind and your subconscious are one of your greatest gifts as a writer, and *this is their finest hour.* For the rest of the journey, they will continue to give you succour. They will still be your engine, but this is the bit where you do your essential maintenance. This is the bit where you fill up with gas, check the tires, and check the water and oil before you turn on the ignition. If you don't do it, you're at serious risk of breaking down midway through your journey.

And why wouldn't you do it? This is the fun part. You're not chained to the desk or your computer. You can do this thinking anywhere. And I do mean, literally, anywhere. All you need is a bit of peace and quiet and the space to think. Park, beach, café, mountainside, pub, strolling through a cemetery. Anywhere where you can just create a bit of headspace and let thoughts and ideas appear to fill the void.

When you've considered your story sufficiently, probed every angle, left no stone unturned and exhausted every avenue, then you're ready to sit yourself down and start writing. Then you can begin.

Just don't underestimate the time you spend thinking about your project.

For me, there are only ever three stages involved in creating a finished product: the idea, the daydreaming, and then the writing.

I should probably add a fourth, which would be editing the text, but editing is really just part of the writing, so let's leave it as three ingredients.

Have an idea.

Explore all of its possibilities.

Then get it written.

That's your one, two, and three.

And remember to enjoy the daydreaming part.

There's an old cartoon caption that says, 'typists type, writers stare out the window.'

Except we don't.

We stare out the window as we daydream, and then we go and write.

HOW TO GET AN AGENT

So let's talk about that mythical, magical beast… the literary agent. How do we get one? Do we really need one? What is it that they do, and what can they do for you?

The first thing to say is that I don't have an agent. Yet! I've never had one. Still, I know a little about the subject, enough to write this chapter, I think, and I hope that you'll find it worthwhile to hear what I have to say.

I managed to get my first two book deals by approaching publishers directly. Whatever else you read in the next 1,000 words or so, always remember that you will always be your own best agent. No one cares about you – or your writing – as much as you do yourself. That will always be true. Never be afraid to fight your own corner and stand your ground, even in the presence of more experienced and knowledgeable people.

Literary agents are deal-makers in the publishing world. They can get your work to all the right people. They have a foot in the door of the leading publishing and production houses. They *know* people.

They act as gatekeepers, in a way; a necessary filter between us writers and the titans of the industry. The good news is, they *need* us. They really do. They only make a living on a percentage of *our* earnings. That percentage is usually between ten and 20 percent. A lot of them split the difference and will settle at 15.

Their names and addresses (business, not personal) can be found in the Writers' and Artists' Yearbook. You can also go to the website for a particular agency and find more in-depth information there, including what each individual agent is interested in and is looking for.

Here's the important part. Don't just send your stuff out willy-nilly. A scattergun approach will not do you any favours. It will be a waste of your time, and you'll also antagonise the agent concerned if they're not right for your work.

Instead, take a deep breath, and spend a lovely day reading about which agencies specialise in your type of writing. Some want fiction, some only non-fiction. Some want children's stories. Some want literary fiction, romance, or sci-fi. Some specialise in screenplays. Some of them, plays.

Grab yourself a pen and a pad and write down a list from the hundreds listed in the *Writers' and Artists' Yearbook* who are interested in the kind of thing that you write or have written.

You *know* what it is that you've created. Presumably, you are searching for an agent to represent a tangible product, i.e., something that you've already written.

You can't write to an agent and say, 'I'm thinking of being a writer. I reckon I'll write a good novel in the next few years. Fancy representing me?'

That's not going to work. It's off to the mad-house with you.

But, imagine you've just completed your manuscript. You might have carried it around in your head for a couple of months or even a couple of years, and then you spent a great deal of time getting it down on paper (or on the computer). And you're really proud of it. It is everything that you hoped it would be. In fact, you even *believe* in it!

The good news is, this is the perfect time to approach those agents. The ones whose names you wrote down on your pad of paper.

This can't be every agent in the book, because some of them won't represent your kind of writing.

Don't try to change their minds. You're not their career-advisor. There will still be plenty of agents listed who represent your genre or type of writing. They will know the market. They will know the value of that market at that particular time.

There are about 160 agents listed in the latest edition of the *Writers' and Artists' Yearbook*. And that's just the UK ones. There are many more listed for overseas.

Imagine if you go to each of those agency websites, and each has between five and ten literary agents on their books, that's about 1,000 agents that you could approach. Except you can't, because they will all have their particular likes and wants. The children's book agent, the crime writing agent, the romance writer's agent, and so on. You might find 40 or 50 that specialise in the kind of book (assuming it's a book) that you've written.

Write all of their names and contact details down on your writing pad. Check the submission guidelines.

Very important, that one.

Don't fall at the final hurdle. If they want a covering letter, a synopsis (i.e., a brief outline) of the whole story, and the first three chapters or the first 10,000 words, then that's what you should send them. Don't think (too much) outside of the box at this point. Follow the instructions. They're there for a reason.

The reason is that these are busy people, whose working week is already full dealing with their existing client list, the writers who are already helping pay their mortgages. Do you think they are going to drop those people for you? When you become one of those big-buck earning clients, will you want your agent to dispense with your needs to go look after an ill-equipped enquiry? No way. So be professional in your approach, follow *their* rules. Do what is asked of you. For now.

And don't just fire off your enquiry to every name on the list in one go. And don't send your email out as a circular or a multi-recipient attachment. Choose, say, five at a time. Choose your favourites first, or do them in alphabetical order. Five at a time. Give them a couple of weeks to reply. See if anyone wants to read any more of your work. If so, then great. If not, move on to the next five.

If, after you've contacted maybe 20 or more of these agents, and you've had nothing positive back, then perhaps your work isn't quite ready. It could be time to shelve it and move on to your next project.

The important thing to note is that, by following their guidelines and submitting in a courteous and professional manner, you can breach their fortress and get them to consider your work.

If it truly has merit, they will get back in touch with you. They honestly want nothing more than to have something land on their desk that blows them away. They want to get excited. They want to see pound signs. They want to imagine getting their hands on the 15 percent of the pile of money that you, the writer, are going to earn.

Remember, 85 percent of £10,000 is better than a hundred percent of £1,000. If you can acquire the services of an agent, go for it. They will be an advisor, an advocate, a champion, counsellor, and possibly friend. They know who's out there looking for just your kind of writing. They know what the market is paying at that time for that type of work. They can help you. They want to. They also love writing. Let's hope they love yours.

And don't just say yes if an agent offers you a deal. This is, hopefully, a long-term relationship. Do you get on? Are they right for you? Do you like each other? Can you work together?

They'll also want to know that you are dedicated to your craft. Are you a one-hit-wonder? Are you a serial writer?

What is your next project, they'll want to know, because they might well find themselves negotiating a two-book deal on your behalf. It would be nice for them to know that you intend to write one.

To sum up, I would say that you first need to finish your book, (and by finish, I mean edit it too) and then approach only the agents that are appropriate for that kind of work. Approach them only in the manner that they have specified, e.g., via email, number of chapters, covering letter, etc. Then, if you're lucky enough to be offered representation, choose someone that you can honestly see yourself working with, and hopefully for a very long time.

And how best to get a literary agent?

Write an amazing book.

HOW TO GET A PUBLISHER

Thanks to the advent of eBooks and the self-publishing opportunities that exist (of which more in the next chapter), what once seemed like a closed shop is now very much open for business. Traditional publishers are in flux. The times really are a-changing, and that's good news for writers.

Previously, the publishing world appeared out of reach for most mere mortals. The workings of publishers were a mystery, and their hallowed halls were not for the likes of us. Occasionally, some lucky author would breach their barricades and disappear through the gilded portal before later reappearing on the other side, bedecked in fame and fortune, and almost unrecognisable from the struggling artist they had been for all of the years leading up to their anointment.

No one knew how they had overcome that seemingly insurmountable hurdle, except I can guarantee that their success involved two key ingredients. They had persistence, and they had a product.

After the best part of three decades, I myself finally managed to breach the same barricades. How did I do it? I followed the advice given in the previous chapter and did the exact same thing.

I took out my *Writers' and Artists' Yearbook*, I went to the chapter on Publishers. I wrote down the contact details for every publisher of non-fiction, leaving out all of those who stated that they were not open for submissions. I was left with a list of about 50 companies that I could approach.

Five at a time, I sent each of them an email titled 'Two best-selling non-fiction books', which was sure to grab their attention and which was, luckily, the truth.

I then told them a little bit about myself and said that I believed I was ready for 'proper' publication, and would they be interested? I told them about the two books I had written, which had made it into the top-five on Amazon in their particular subject. I also gave them a copy of my literary CV.

The result? Lots of positive feedback, and ultimately two book publishing deals.

Now, these people didn't just say 'thanks for your email. Here's a book publishing deal'. No. We talked. We had email exchanges and spoke on the phone.

One of the publishers read my CV and spotted a play that I had written. They suggested a book on the same subject. Of course, I said yes.

The other deal was for one of my pre-existing tomes, one of the ones that I'd talked up in my initial email. It was high in the Amazon charts for sales and reviews. In one month alone, that particular book had earned me £1,000. And that was at £1 a copy. Sales were 1,000 for a single calendar month. Not a bad return (in truth, my best ever!), and it made those publishers sit up and take notice.

So, whilst it wasn't as simple as just sending an email, and there were further negotiations required, at least I had a foot in the door. These people were talking to me. We worked it out and got there in the end.

Neither of the publishing deals were with major publishing houses. These were more bespoke, independent players. I wasn't being offered huge advances. There was no talk of giving up the day job just yet. But these were professional and respectable publishers. They both offered me a deal. And I accepted.

So, do your research, approach them in a manner in which they wish to be approached, and do the deal as professionally as you would in any other area of your life. Don't get flummoxed because the dream you've held for all of your adult life is about to come true. This is business. Nice business, but business all the same.

Get the deal out of the way, and then you can get back to your writing.

Publishers are more approachable than they have ever been before. You can find them on the internet, on Twitter, or in the *Writers' and Artists' Yearbook*.

Once you have something of merit, make the call or send that email. Or, like I did, think of your self-published eBook as an advance publicity campaign for the major publishing deal you hope to sign.

If – and when – you do get published, you'll benefit from all of their editorial and marketing expertise. And you'll be a writer of a different ilk. Somehow validated. You'll probably feel like you've reached the top of a very high mountain. You'll probably give yourself a pat on the back and say to yourself, 'I did it!' And rightly so.

Publishers need writers, without whom they have no product. Their fortress walls have never been more vulnerable.

So go storm the barricades!

SELF-PUBLISHING

There are none so mad as the self-produced or the self-published. At least, that's the way it used to be. Now, independent authors are the vanguard of a new publishing phenomenon. Your work can be made as widely available as that of the most successful and well-resourced writers in the world.

Amazon (though there are other platforms available) walk you through the process of uploading your latest book. It is quick and easy to do, taking little more than an hour or so. By the following day, your work will be available for sale across the globe.

You set the price that you want to sell at. You are, to all intents and purposes, your own publisher. You might want to stand out from the crowd by getting a professional book cover made. I use a friend who is a graphic designer. I usually pay him about £100.

Again, Amazon is there to talk you through the process of uploading the cover: the ideal size and the number of pixels required, that sort of thing.

Despite being very much a technophobe, I've managed to self-publish two works of fiction and four of non-fiction. If you have a book to take to market, just follow the instructions, upload the text and cover, set the rate that you want to sell at, and away you go.

There are a few formatting issues that you need to pay attention to. These are a little tricky, at first, but it shouldn't take you more than half a day to format your entire text to make it both print and eBook friendly.

Apparently, the machines at work on your book don't take too kindly to tab indentations and a few other things, such as italics. You just need to spend a few hours making your text robot-friendly, and then you can upload it.

You are also able to review the text before it is fully uploaded, so if you have made a few layout errors, you can go back in and make those further changes. It's very user-friendly, especially for the nervous amateur amongst us.

And then you are a (self) published author.

People can buy your book as easily as they can buy the latest Stephen King book or the latest Lee Child. You're competing with the best of them.

The difficult thing with fiction is that you're competing with about a million other books, so unless you get lucky and somehow grab the attention of the reading public, your books will probably never be found amongst the myriad available.

You want (and need) to get some reviews up there. Maybe give your book away for free for a few weeks to try and entice readers, or maybe price low, or price promote. I really don't know the answer as my own works of fiction are languishing in terms of sales. It's a very crowded marketplace.

When it comes to non-fiction, things get a little easier. If you were to search for a book on Israel and Palestine, I show up in the top five, and that's from over 10,000 results. How many pages of search results are people going to trawl through to find a book that they want to read? My guess is two or three at the most. Being on that first results page means that your book will be easily found.

And if you do self-publish a book, just think of it as an advance publicity campaign for the professional publishing campaign that you hope will follow.

The advantages of self-publishing are so great that many authors – even after they've been offered that Holy Grail professional publishing deal – decide to continue on the self-publishing road. It really is that good.

There is no longer any stigma to being self-published. There used to be something called vanity publishing, which was self-publishing in a former life.

It involved publishers, usually no more than glorified printers, offering their services to people who had little hope in hell of getting a proper publishing deal. Hence the 'vanity' part of the name.

That's all gone. We exist on another plane now. You can hold your head up very high indeed as a self-published author. Like I say, some people give up that mantle very reluctantly, even when offered all sorts of incentives to do so.

Of course, being self-published means that you are your own editor, typesetter, agent, publicist, etc., and you miss out on the professional support that an established publishing house can bring you, but at least it gives you the opportunity to put your work out there. That's all most of us are really aiming for.

We want to be read, and then we hope that the feedback will be positive, and then we wait to see what opportunities might follow on the back of that. A bit of cash for all of our efforts wouldn't go amiss either.

Amazon take between 30 and 65% of the sale price (the price that *you* set) for their services (depending on what publishing options you choose). That means that you, the writer, get the remainder. With a Kindle book, for example, if you market your book at a tenner, then that means you make around seven pounds for every book sold. For a hard copy version of the same book, you'd get £3.50.

Now ten pounds is not unreasonable for a non-fiction title, but most works of fiction sell for a lot less. Even the bestselling titles usually cost little more than a fiver, especially for the electronic versions.

That's understandable. EBooks cost nothing in terms of printing and distribution. They don't need to be stored in warehouses or distributed in vans to bookstores across the land. They're not a tangible product. They're just part of that spiritual ether that is the internet.

If you choose to go down the self-publishing route, you are going to bypass all of the gate-keepers that usually judge your book's quality. The market, or the lack of one, will be the ultimate arbiter of your work.

As far as I'm aware, there are no rules concerning the quality of what you can upload. You could even publish your weekly shopping list if you wanted to. But would anyone want to buy it or read it? I very much doubt it.

So, whether you are approaching professional publishers or have decided to self-publish yourself, remember to write to the best of your ability. Don't dumb down just because no-one might ever read it. Instead, think of it as your advance marketing campaign for the professional publishing to come.

Right now, publishers are flummoxed. Go get them while their defences are down.

LEARN TO TYPE

Quentin Tarantino once said that you can't write poetry on a computer. I guess some people still prefer to write with pen and paper, especially when writing that first draft. But, ultimately, those words will need to be committed into a form where it can be made available for distribution, by which I mean a document or a typed-up script.

I can write a play, and maybe even a screenplay, with pen and paper. However, a novel is a different proposition. Do you really want to re-write 100,000 words? I don't think so.

When you come to tackle a major piece of writing, you're probably going to do it on a computer. As one student of writing once said, 'When I'm writing at the computer, I'm writing all the time. It's not re-writing or re-typing.'

I'd agree with that, and I guess the same will be true for you.

When you're writing, you're tapping into your subconscious. Assuming you have followed the guidelines in this book, hopefully you've built up some sort of writing routine.

Once you've established that routine, your subconscious will be a valuable resource, and it will be available to you on tap.

Now, something is going to act as a conduit between your subconscious and those words on the screen. That something is you. You're the cipher, the translator.

Your subconscious isn't going to make those words appear on the page. You have to do that part yourself.

How well do you type? If you have to stop and search for every single letter that you put down, that is going to dull the senses and use up brainpower that you need to reserve for your writing.

So, learn to type. Or, at least, learn to type a bit faster.

I've never done a typing course, but I've written that many words down, over the years, that I can now type 30 or 40 words a minute. I get into a rhythm. I don't need to check where I'm going.

The odd spelling mistake gets picked up by the spell-checker anyway, and I can go back and make corrections when I get a break in the writing. By not worrying about making mistakes, I can keep on going. I can probably write about 1,000 words in an hour. That's pretty good.

A professional typist might reach 100 words a minute. We don't need to do that. We're writers, not typists.

If you want to take a typing course, I would say, good on you. If not, I would say that you should at least try to improve your output.

The less time you spend looking for letters on the keyboard, the more time you have to write. The easier you hit those letters on the keyboard, the less you disturb your brain and subconscious from their primary function, which is to serve up your story to you.

Typists type. Writers stare out windows. And then type.

The better we are at getting those words down on paper, the more productive and prolific we will be.

Learn to type, or at least improve your typing skills. You're going to be doing an awful lot of it.

So you may as well try to do it well.

THE WRITER'S GUILD.
YOUR UNION

Did you know that you have a union? Yes, lonely, independent writers have a union that is available to us. One that understands us. Indeed, one that exists just for us.

The Writers' Guild of Great Britain (WGGB) celebrated, in 2019, 60 years of representing writers. It is a trade union that looks after authors working in television, film, theatre, radio, literature, poetry, comedy, animation, and video games.

As well as professionals, it also serves the needs of both emerging and aspiring writers. They negotiate for better pay and working conditions, and lobby and campaign on behalf of all writers.

Full membership costs about £200 a year, while fees for those just starting in the industry, or yet to earn a professional income from their writing, come in at just over £100.

They used to publish a monthly magazine that was full of interesting articles and handy tips. They've now gone online with this, and publish a weekly newsletter.

There is also a separate body called the Alliance of Independent Authors, which deals with writers primarily involved in the area of self-publishing.

Both organisations are there to lend support to writers who don't operate in a conventional workplace and are without colleagues as such, and who therefore don't usually have access to information or guidance from their peers.

WGGB can offer advice on contracts and fees, intervene in disputes, and offer a whole host of other services, including free and discounted training, social events, and inclusion in its 'Find a Writer' directory.

If you ever feel, as a writer, that you would benefit from inclusion in a trade union or even in a community of like-minded individuals, then it's good to know that such places do exist.

I've previously been a member, and enjoyed the feeling that I was somehow now part of 'the industry'. If you can afford to join, I would heartily recommend it.

I'll be back there myself very soon.

COPYRIGHT. PROTECT YOURSELF

You can't copyright ideas.

Imagine this. You're down the pub with a mate and say, 'I'd love to write a detective series set in modern-day London.' Then, you proceed to get drunk. Then, six months later, your (so-called) friend says they've just sold a script to ITV for a cop show set in modern-day London. Does that mean that they nicked your idea?

Probably.

Can you do anything about it?

Not a damn thing. Because you can't copyright ideas.

What you can copyright is a tangible product, e.g., a script or manuscript. If you can prove that something exists and that you created it, then the copyright rests with you. Copyright is inherent in the product's creator.

Copyright rests in the physical expression of the idea, not in the idea itself.

So, it isn't enough to have formulated the idea; you must then express it in a tangible form such as a play, film script, or novel. Now, you have something that you can point to and say, 'I did that'. Now, if someone else copies it or tries to claim ownership, you can point to its existence, and even better if you can point out the fact that you emailed it (say to your work email address) prior to any date that your opponent (for want of a better word) can prove any ownership.

In days of yore, writers like myself would spend precious pounds posting sealed envelopes containing our original scripts back to ourselves. When they were delivered, we would place them in a filing cabinet or drawer at home, ready for any possible future court case should someone wish to take the credit and subsequent riches from our masterpieces. Nowadays, just email yourself a copy.

And if you ever wish to use the work of someone else, someone who is the author of the piece and the owner of the copyright, then please treat that person as you would wish to be treated yourself.

If you've read a good book and you think it would make a good play or film, then ask yourself a simple question: is the book still in copyright?

Copyright lasts for 70 years from the end of the calendar year in which the author died. If you're adapting *Frankenstein*, then you don't have a problem, as long as you're writing an original adaptation based on the original material. If you want to do the National Theatre's version of

Frankenstein, their version will have its own copyright. And so will yours, as long as you do your own version based purely on Mary Shelley's book.

If you want to use or work from a more recent text, or one where the author died less than 70 years before you plan to produce your work, then you need to contact the estate of the deceased writer or find out who owns the copyright, which will involve a bit of research. Then you need to come to some arrangement or agreement with the holders of the rights. Then you're good to go.

As soon as you have expressed your own idea in tangible form, the copyright automatically belongs to you. You *own* it. You created something from nothing. It's not just a good idea or even a good afternoon in the pub with your mate. You are the official holder of the copyright of a novel, play, or screenplay. It belongs to you.

Copyright is your friend. It protects the author from the unscrupulous and the downright greedy. It can be a bit of a grey area but, ultimately, if you wrote it, you own it.

As Ghandi, a former lawyer himself, once said, 'If you are in the right, nine times out of ten, the law will come to your aid.'

TWENTY YEARS TO BECOME AN OVERNIGHT SUCCESS

Let's be honest, most of us, even though we write because we are natural-born storytellers, still imagine what wealth and opportunities might come our way. We want to be successful in what we do.

There's no shame in admitting as much. The reality is, and I'm certainly speaking for myself here, I would like nothing better than to wake up in the morning and go to the computer and write stories all day. I believe I'd put in as many hours and be as hard-working as I would in any day job. I would, however, be doing something I truly loved: sharing my stories with the world.

But then reality kicks in. Will I earn enough as a writer to pay the rent and bills at the end of the month?

I hope that you'll find the success that your talent deserves. I also hope that you'll enjoy a happy and fulfilling life. Remember, success is a journey, not a destination. I'll say it again. Success is a journey, not a destination.

The reason for the repeat is that I'd heard it before and never really got it, until my hopes of becoming an overnight success in years one, two, and three, and all the way up to approaching 30, came to be the truth of my life. Was I a good person? Did I value my friends and family and earn their esteem in return? Or was I simply marking time before I disappeared into, and onto, a different plane?

Your early writing years will be learning ones. At least, that is how it will be for most of us mere mortals. Then, life and its inherent responsibilities – plus your own social and familial wants and needs – will rear their heads and demand that you pay attention. Then, if you're still serious about being a writer (as I sincerely hope you are), you'll keep writing, but you may find that the hours in which you do so are limited and you'll have to be more disciplined than ever.

All of that endeavour, perseverance, and continued professional development will ultimately see you break down the barricades. You get that book deal, that play, or those ten plays performed. You've got a body of work. You've built up some reputation and maybe even a loyal following. Other people will catch on. They'll say that this guy, or girl, is good. You should check them out.

You approach that agent or publisher. You tell them what you've done to date. They can't *believe* that no one has snapped you up before now. Guess what. Your time has just come.

Be that after ten, 20, or 30 years, if you've put the hours in, you'll be ready for the opportunity that life and the writing industry is about to present to you.

And you'll have earned it. And I wish you good luck. Just don't forget, it's a journey, and not a destination.

SO YOU WANT TO RETIRE EARLY?

The truth is, you can't. And why would you want to? If you do something that you absolutely love, you never really do a day's work in your life.

But I suppose that's still a dream that many of us share, to be able to give up the day job and go and write every day. Is that retirement? Not really, except in the sense that you're not really working because you are doing something that you would be happy to do anyway, unprompted and unpaid. Because we are storytellers.

The best stories are the ones we believe in. Brad Meltzer, author, said that. I think that's true for both the writer and the reader. It will certainly improve the quality of your writing and imbue it with passion if you believe what you are writing.

Maybe that's what we mean by retiring early, simply finding the time available to tell the stories we wish to tell. Doesn't sound like a bad idea, does it?

I don't think any of us want to retire from writing. I think, what we really want at the end of a long, happy, and productive life is to lie in perpetuity beneath a gravestone bearing the words 'Here lies a storyteller', accompanied by all the other important stuff along the lines of 'beloved husband, father, brother, son, and friend, etc.'.

You'll need a bit of cash to support your lifestyle when you give up work anyway. Writing can be a good second income, or even your bread and butter and possibly – though rarely – your champagne and caviar too.

Hopefully, by the time you reach an age where you are ready and able to slow down, you'll have learned how to master the market and to draw financial succour from its available income streams.

The good thing for us, as writers, is that we can work from the comfort of our homes. The work isn't physically demanding and, therefore, the ageing process will have little impact on our talents. And, if you are earning a decent income from your writing, that income is tax-deductible.

The fact that you are working from home, and earning your income from there, means that you can also offset a portion of your household expenditure, including your rent or mortgage, and your household bills including your gas and electricity, phone, internet, etc. That's a pretty good incentive to keep writing and keep on earning.

So, want to retire early? You can't. Not really. But then, you wouldn't want to anyway, because you're a writer.

MARKETING YOURSELF AND YOUR WORK

There's a lot of competition out there. You're in competition with me. I'm in competition with you. And we're all in competition with everything else that tries to attract the attention of the viewing and reading, the watching and listening public.

There's no better advertising than word of mouth. If you can create an exciting, original, interesting product, then hopefully those who find you first will start the ball rolling for you. Even then, you still need to generate as much publicity and traction for the work you've laboured over for so long.

Do you have a social media profile? Do you use it? Do you use it well, or enough?

Whenever I have a new play on, or a new book to promote, I contact my local radio stations and newspapers and ask if they'd like to do an interview with little old me, a local writer. More times than not, they say yes.

Harold Robbins, one of the 20th Century's bestselling authors, was no shrinking violet. Obviously, he was a master storyteller (*A Stone for Danny Fisher* remains one of my all-time favourite books), but he was also a master of self-promotion. In his own words, he once said, 'I've banged the drum a bit more than most'.

That's what you have to do. Bang the drum for your work (or for yourself if you feel so inclined).

People I know feel that I have an almost shame-faced gift for self-promotion. The thing is, I've only ever got up there – and out there – when I had something to promote. I don't promote *me* as a writer. I wouldn't dream of it. What I get out there and shout about is the product.

If I've got a play showing somewhere, then I am duty-bound to get out there and tell everyone about it. I always say, I can shout it from the rooftops (and I practically do) because I know that no-one is going away disappointed.

Believe me, if I thought the product was rubbish, I would keep schtum about it. Instead, if I believe that you will love or like my latest offering, I will walk the streets delivering flyers (professionally designed and printed) through the letterbox of your home to try and entice you along.

I was once asked, after personally posting 20,000 flyers through letterboxes ahead of a forthcoming play, if something as old-fashioned as that actually works.

The answer is, of course it does. It *all* works. Anything that you can do to let people know of a forthcoming event *works*.

Go down to your local pub and stand at the bar. Bump into a few old friends. They know you're a writer. They're bound to ask what you're working on at the moment.

'I have a play on at the such-and-such theatre next week,' you say.

Guess what? You may have just sold a few tickets.

And when they're in work that week, and their colleagues ask them what they have planned for the weekend, they'll mention that they're going to see a play written by a friend. Now *they're* interested too. You just sold a few more tickets.

Agents, publishers, producers, and the like will all want to know that you can meet them halfway and generate at least some publicity for the thing that you're asking them to support.

You can't just say 'Here's the script. Go make me a fortune'. It's best that you get involved and back your own product.

Bang the drum. Bang it loud.

Standing at a bus stop. Sitting on the bus. Everywhere and everyone is an opportunity.

Don't go running naked across the pitch in the middle of a Premiership match with the name of your new book or play emblazoned across your bare chest, though. Try to keep a bit of decorum. But flyering, chatting to people, doing interviews with the media, posting on social media. These are all legitimate forms of advertising.

If a tree falls in the forest, does anyone hear it? If you write a masterpiece and don't show it to anyone, or tell anyone that it's on at the theatre down the road next week, will anyone hear that too?

For my first self-published work, I held a book launch at my local pub. About 50 people turned up. I sold about 35 copies at a tenner apiece. That was £350 (which I passed to my mother at the next table to pay off a small portion of my debt to that incredible and supportive woman).

A room in a back-street pub in Liverpool generated that amount of interest and support from my family and friends.

A couple of weeks later, I read an article in the Independent newspaper. One of their regular columnists had just published a book. His book-launch and signing was held in a branch of Waterstones near Oxford Street in Central London.

His book sales that day? Eight copies. His publisher, he lamented in his column the following week, asked him if he didn't have any friends or family that he could have invited along.

I know which one I'd have expected to yield the greater results: a backstreet pub versus a central branch of a major bookstore. Just goes to show. You're your own best publicist and promoter. You can't afford to be shy.

Just make sure, if you are shouting it from the rooftops, that you have something worthwhile to show them. Otherwise, you'll be known as the boy (or girl) who cried wolf.

Ultimately, your work deserves an audience. Or, at least, it does when you're ready as a writer.

You owe it to yourself to make it available to the people who might be interested, engaged, enthused, and maybe even blown away by your work.

You're a writer. Go write. And when you're ready, go find your audience.

Thanks for listening.

The best of luck.

CONCLUSION

It's 30 years now since I said those magic words, 'I want to be a writer'. And guess what? They are as true now as they were then. I still want to be a writer.

I know I *am* a writer, but I don't do it for a living. Not yet. I still have to work. I still can't just wake up every morning and go write. So I write, but I'm not a full-time writer. It's still a dream and a goal. And I'm getting there.

Each completed project is a step along the way, another box ticked, more apprentice-hours served. I'm improving. Hopefully getting good feedback. Maybe getting a little attention, building up a fan-base, earning a bit of money. Putting in those 20 years of labour to become an overnight success. Or for as long or a short as it takes.

It's all there for you. You want to be a writer. All you have to do is write. Talent and perseverance. That's all it really takes. If you get a lucky break with your first novel, was that really a lucky break if you still don't know what you're doing? How are you going to follow up with book number two? You could see your hopes (and your reputation) dashed if you haven't got that solid foundation that comes with learning your craft.

Because writing is a craft. As much as needlework or stone-masonry. It's a craft you have to learn. And the more you practice, the better you'll become.

You're creating art. That makes you an artist. Sounds good, doesn't it? Feels good too.

This might just be your hobby, or it could be your calling in life. You need to put your talent on the page, and then show that work to someone to gauge its worth. You need to keep going. Talent and perseverance.

Ultimately, our dreams can come true, because the world needs stories, and stories need writers.

Imagine holding that published book in your hands, or seeing the crowd on their feet cheering your hit play. That's where you're headed. That's what you want to achieve.

And you're allowed to dream, and you're allowed to believe, because you're a writer. We create stories, and that includes our own.

So you want to be a writer? What are you waiting for? Go write!

THE END

OTHER BOOKS FROM BENNION KEARNY

From the author of this book

Israel and Palestine: The Complete History [2019 Edition]

Israel and Palestine: The Complete History seeks to explain the overall story of Israeli and Palestinian tensions and divisions in the region. Indeed, without properly understanding the full history of the area, it is impossible to understand the current situation.

In this book, author Ian Carroll takes the reader back to the very beginning of the conflict some 4,000 years ago, then moves through the major events of the Middle Ages and 20th century, and brings us right up to the present day, documenting the significant events that have happened along the way. The reader is allowed to make up their own mind as to where praise and condemnation belong with this complicated issue.

From Exodus to the birth of Jesus, from Islam to the Crusades, through the Diaspora and up to the recreation of the modern state of Israel and beyond, Israel and Palestine: The Complete History avoids a dry academic approach. It aims to tell the history of the region and peoples in a balanced and brisk fashion, from a storyteller's perspective.

Write From The Start: The Beginner's Guide to Writing Professional Non-Fiction by Caroline Foster

Write From The Start is a book that is aimed at novice writers, hobbyist writers, or those considering a full-time writing career, and offers a comprehensive guide to help readers plan, prepare, and professionally submit their non-fiction work.

It is designed to get people up-and-running fast. *Write From The Start* teaches how to explore topic areas methodically, tailor content for different audiences, and create compelling copy.

It will teach readers which writing styles work best for specific publications, how to improve one's chances of securing both commissioned and uncommissioned work, how to build a portfolio that gets results, and how to take that book idea all the way to publication.

Togetherness: How to Build a Winning Team by Dr Matt Slater

Togetherness is a powerful state of connection between individuals that can lead to amazing triumphs. In sport, teams win matches, but teams with togetherness win championships and make history.

If you want the individuals on your team to develop their skills and reach their potential, get them 'together'. The key to this, is to understand your players' group memberships and how to harness them, to create a unique team identity that is special to "us".

This concise and practical book – from Dr. Matt Slater, a world authority on togetherness – shows you how you can develop togetherness in your team. The journey starts with an understanding of what underpins togetherness and how it can drive high performance and well-being simultaneously. It then moves onto practical tips and activities based on the 3R model (Reflect, Represent, Realise) that you can learn and complete with your team to unlock their togetherness.